STEWARDSHIP ILLUSTRATIONS

LIBRARY OF CHRISTIAN STEWARDSHIP

STEWARDSHIP ILLUSTRATIONS

edited by
T. K. Thompson

UNITY SCHOOL LIBRARY
DISCARD
Lee's Su ... ssouri 64063

Prentice-Hall, Inc., Englewood Cliffs, N. J.

© 1965 by Prentice-Hall, Inc., Englewood Cliffs, N. J.

All rights reserved including the right to reproduce this book, or any portions thereof, in any form, except for the inclusion of brief quotations in a review.

Library of Congress Catalog Card Number: 65-16587
Printed in the United States of America
T 84654 (paper)   T 84655 (case)

Prentice-Hall International, Inc., *London*
Prentice-Hall of Australia, Pty., Ltd., *Sydney*
Prentice-Hall of Canada, Ltd., *Toronto*
Prentice-Hall of India (Private) Ltd., *New Delhi*
Prentice-Hall of Japan, Inc., *Tokyo*

BV
772
.T49

ACKNOWLEDGMENTS

Grateful acknowledgment is made to the following publishers, agents, authors and copyright owners for permission to reprint in this volume from the works listed below (with cross reference to our illustration number):

Abingdon Press for *The Stewardship Life* by Julius Earl Crawford (113).

George Allen & Unwin, Ltd. for *Philanthropy in England, 1480-1660* by W. K. Jordan (114).

Association Press for *Archaeology of the New Testament* by Roland Kenneth Harrison (42, 80, 81).

Baker Book House for *Story of Stewardship* by George A. E. Salstrand (9).

Beacon Hill Press for *Treasury of Stewardship Illustrations* by Basil Miller. Used by permission (12, 68, 90).

The Bethany Press for *Financing Faith* by Harriet Harmon Dexter (77, 102, 107); *Finding Holy Ground* by Harold L. Lunger (19); and *A God to Glorify* by Jack V. Reeve (27).

Burns & MacEachern Ltd. for *The Other Six Days* by Dr. Joseph C. McLelland (6, 15).

Funk & Wagnalls Company, Inc. and Mrs. Rebecca B. King for *Successful Fund-Raising Sermons* by Julius King (38).

The Geneva Press, Saturday Review and Norman Cousins for *Servants and Stewards* by Arthur McKay, © 1963 by W. L. Jenkins. Used by permission (41).

Harcourt, Brace & World, Inc. for *Wind, Sand and Stars* by Antoine de Saint-Exupèry (106).

Harper & Row, Publishers for *Laughing Stewardship Through* by Guy L. Morrill (1, 2, 3, 10, 28, 40, 45, 73, 116, 117); *The Finances of a Church* by Robert Cashman (24); and *Twelve Baskets Full* by Margaret T. Applegarth (23, 25).

John Knox Press for *The Meaning of Gifts* by Paul Tournier (33).

Koinonia Community for *Why Jan Did Not Graduate* from Koinonia Newsletter #29, dated September 15, 1964 (70).

The Macmillan Company for *The Sword and the Cross* by Robert M. Grant (110).

Mennonite Publishing House for *The Challenge of Christian Stewardship* by Milo Kauffman (36).

The Methodist Church (Board of Missions and Church Education) for *The Fine Art of Using* by Dr. Ralph W. Sockman, 1946. Used by permission (47, 54, 98, 100, 101).

The Methodist Story for *Our World in Miniature* by Henry Smith Leiper, issue dated November, 1963 (112).

The Missouri Synod of the Lutheran Church for *Five Grains of Corn*, a letter to members (30).

A. R. Mowbray & Co. Ltd. for *Moral Theology in the Modern World* by Lindsay Dewar. Used by permission (29).

Nazarene Publishing House for *Treasures in Heaven* by M. Lunn. Used by permission (13, 48).

The Presbyterian Foundation, Inc. (U. S.) for *Any Old Stock in Your Attic* from *The Christian Will*, vol. VI, No. 1 published November, 1963 (34).

Fleming H. Revell Company for *Turbulent World, Tranquil God* by Reuben K. Youngdahl. Used by permission (11).

Charles Scribner's Sons for *John D. Rockefeller: A Study in Power* by Allan Nevins (52).

The Seabury Press, Inc. for *Tall in His Presence* by George McNeill Ray (95).

The Sunday School Board of the Southern Baptist Convention for *The Gospel of Giving* by Herschel H. Hobbs (16, 50), and *My Money and God* by Robert J. Hastings (4, 7, 78).

United Church Herald for *First Century Board Meeting* by Theodore A. Braun, issue of October 1, 1964 (64).

United Press International and The Christian Century Foundation for *Death Down a Dark Street* by Dean Peerman, copyright 1963 by Christian Century Foundation and Louis Cassel's UPI release, February 8, 1963 (92).

Warner Press, Inc. for *Our Search for Success* by Rolla O. Swisher, copyright 1963 by Warner Press, Inc. Used by permission (60).

Zondervan Publishing House for *Christian Stewardship and Church Finance* by H. W. Ellis. Used by permission (67, 69).

CONTENTS

INTRODUCTION

LIBRARY OF CHRISTIAN STEWARDSHIP will provide the pastor and stewardship-finance leaders of congregations with needed background materials for a stewardship program.

This volume, *Stewardship Illustrations*, will provide the pastor, church school teacher, canvass chairman, and stewardship leader with a reservoir of brief stories of Christian stewardship in its practical application.

Later volumes will deal with such subjects as motives for Christian giving, communicating Christian stewardship, a stewardship commentary on the Old Testament, a stewardship commentary on the New Testament, and stewardship themes in great literature.

All volumes in the series will be published in both cloth and paper-bound editions. Their convenient and uniform size, attractive format and reasonable price will enable the local church to obtain multiple copies for use in leadership training, group study and program development. The contributors will be recognized authorities in the subject area treated. Popularly written, each book will serve as a reliable guide and ready reference for key leaders in the congregation.

T. K. THOMPSON
General Editor

PREFACE

Stewardship teaching and preaching should be based upon sound biblical exegesis, careful study of church history, a review of the history of the doctrine, and a precise knowledge of the techniques of modern communication. In this stewardship is no different from any of the other great doctrines of the Christian faith.

In stewardship preaching and teaching, there is particular need for concrete, vivid illustration, because stewardship is above all else "the practice of the Christian faith." (Greever). The best sources of illustrations are the Bible and the personal experience of the speaker. The 2,000 years of church history also offer rich sources for illustration.

The editors of the "Library of Christian Stewardship" felt that early in this series there should appear a book of stewardship illustrations, because the field is relatively limited. Some of the best books are now out of print. Some of the literature is in pamphlet or leaflet form, and needs more permanent format. Virtually every pastor and church school teacher deals with stewardship throughout the year.

The plan of this book, *Stewardship Illustrations,* is to present approximately 100 of the best illustrations from stewardship literature of the last 50 years, based upon suggestions received from a group of about 30 stewardship leaders in the

United States and Canada. Those illustrations which passed a critical board of review have been organized into a series of themes, as set forth in the table of contents. The decision as to which category was often quite arbitrary, and many illustrations would serve equally well in two or more classifications.

Some practical notes on the use of the book may be helpful.

1. Read through the entire volume, marking those stories of special appeal. Note in the margin possible cross reference for other themes.

2. A series of stewardship sermons might be based upon ideas contained in the chapter "Sentence Sermons."

3. Use this book in connection with other books in this series, "Library of Christian Stewardship."

4. Note that the basic criteria for the choice of these illustrations was practical application in the life of the Christian.

A special word of thanks is due to the members of the Department of Stewardship and Benevolence of the National Council of Churches who suggested most of these illustrations and to a special panel of critics who evaluated the hundreds of illustrations submitted. A final word of thanks is due the dozens of distinguished ministers who submitted illustrations, not all of which found place in the volume.

T. K. THOMPSON

BUDGETS

1.   BEFORE YOU SPEND

"Before you start," said the photographer, intercepting a channel swimmer, "I should like to get a snapshot of you, landing." A budget does just that; it takes a picture of the dollar landing, before it starts out. A budget is keeping an expense account *before*, instead of *after* you spend.

Guy L. Morrill

2.   THE COST OF LIVING

Too many Christians, like other folks, are figuring their living costs by the following rule:

Gumm: "Do you know any reliable way for estimating the cost of living?"

Dumm: "Yes. Take your income, whatever that may be, and then add ten or fifteen percent."

Guy L. Morrill

3.   DOLLARS AND SENSE

Keeping fit financially is the one chief difficulty of many
people. Their finances are very anaemic or are in the doldrums,
suffering from a bad case of unbalanced disbursement. The finances of most families, as well as of most individuals, need
constant and skilled attention. Great numbers of people need to
learn how to diagnose the symptoms of their money troubles.
Our dollars, like the dollars of other people, must be taught to
have more sense. We must be able to tell each dollar exactly
where we want it to go.

Guy L. Morrill

EXAMPLE

THE STEWARDSHIP OF INFLUENCE

One day when Bobbie Burns was at the height of his popularity he noticed the admiration of a little boy who followed him around. He turned to him and asked, "Walter, what do you want?" The lad answered that some day he, too, would like to be a great writer. Burns laid his hand on the boy's head as he said, "You can be a great writer some day, Walter, and you will be." The boy became Sir Walter Scott; and he was everlastingly grateful for the man who spoke a word of encouragement in season. "A word fitly spoken is like apples of gold in pictures of silver." (Prov. 25:11)

In 1871 the *New York Herald* sent Henry M. Stanley in search of David Livingstone, long overdue from his third trip into Africa. He found the missionary explorer in Ujiji, Central Africa, and spent four months with him. Stanley went to Africa a confirmed atheist, but Livingstone's influence—his piety, gentleness, and zeal—won him over. Stanley became a Christian, saying, "I was converted by him, although he had not tried to do it." Livingstone was a good steward of his daily influence.

Centuries ago a young monk went on a preaching tour with the famed St. Francis of Assisi. But to the young monk's surprise,

St. Francis simply mingled with the people without preaching a single sermon. His explanation, "My child, we were preaching as we walked and talked with people." The stewardship of influence!

Robert J. Hastings

5.   THE UNWRITTEN LAW OF THE WOODS

All through the Adirondack Mountains are well-marked trails. Wherever these trails intersect you will usually find an open hut, known to climbers as a "lean-to."

When you reach a "lean-to" and lay down your heavy pack at the end of a weary day, there is always dry firewood inside the shelter, always soft balsam on which to lay your blankets. No ranger employed by the state has cut this wood or laid the balsam for your bed. The last camper did this before he left.

Ours can be a happy world when we're not preoccupied with our own journey but have a thought for the other men who walk the trail. In the Adirondacks they call this the unwritten law of the woods. In our churches we call it benevolence.

Henry B. Luffberry

6.   LUTHER ON HONEST WORK

Luther is no mere "secularist." He seeks to give these worldly callings their rightful place, and so has practical words to give about their Divine intention:

It is stealing when a man-servant or a maid-servant is unfaithful in duty . . . I may say the same of mechanics, workmen,

and day-laborers, all of whom act wantonly, knowing not how to cheat their employers enough. In like manner dishonesty is rampant and in full force at the market and in everyday business. In barter the one deceives the other with inferior goods, false measures, unjust weights, counterfeit money, dexterous tricks, clever financiering, and plausible tales. Who can mention all the species of fraud? . . . there are also men whom you may call gentlemen-robbers, land-grabbers, and road-agents, quite above the safe-robber or pilferer of petty cash. These occupy seats of honor, are styled great lords and honorable pious citizens, and under the cloak of honesty they rob and steal. Yea, we might well let the lesser individual thieves alone if we could only arrest the great, powerful arch-thieves.
—(Large Catechism)

Joseph C. McLelland

7.   THE LIGHT WE LEAVE BEHIND

Harry Lauder, the Scottish comedian, liked to describe the old lamplighter who came by his boyhood home each evening to light the gas lamps. He would light the lamp in front of Lauder's home, then make his way, back and forth, down the street. In the deepening twilight, the lad would lose sight of the old lamplighter. "But," he explained, "I always knew where he was by the avenue of light he left behind him."

The train of light he left behind! Here is a parable of life. We make our way down the avenue of life, first on one side, then on the other side of the street. Sometimes we run, again we walk. Occasionally we stop to rest. But evening comes and twilight wraps its purple mantle around our shoulders. Then it is dark. But our friends, our loved ones, have an unmistakable indication of where we are going by the light we leave behind. The wise use of money, in life and in death, is but one of many ways of letting our light shine.

Robert J. Hastings

8.   A SON'S INFLUENCE

Nearing the climax of the first every-member canvass this church had experienced, a married son said to his father, a widely known official of the church, "Aren't you going to give more than 25¢ weekly for the coming year?" He went on to say, "My wife and I have prayed earnestly about what we should give to the church. You know we owe on our farm and we're keeping the kids in school; but we're going to attempt $6.00 per week. Dad," continued the son, "your farm is paid for and your children are all grown. Surely you want to give more for the work of the church than 25¢ a week!"

The pastor who told me this reported that before the canvass was concluded, the older man accepted his son's challenge and made a commitment of $3.00 weekly, which represented a twelve-fold increase over his former giving.

Harl L. Russell

9.   JUDSON'S STEWARDSHIP

The spirit of sacrifice on the part of missionaries was a vital factor in promoting the idea of stewardship in the early part of the nineteenth century. Adoniram Judson, the American Baptist missionary pioneer to Burma, serves as an example. Judson held that his life belonged to the missionary cause on the basis that it provided his living. He retained nothing of the considerable funds that came to him from other sources such as money received from the British government for invaluable service rendered as an interpreter and translator. In 1828 he wrote to the Triennial Convention renouncing his possessions and turning them over to the board. He explained in the letter that when he left America he had in his possession a considerable sum of money consisting of personal earnings as well as gifts of relatives and friends. The money accumulated interest for many years and with occasional accessions from other quarters it now amounted to twelve thousand rupees or six thousand dollars. Judson wrote: "I beg now to present it to the board, or rather to Him that loved us and washed us from our sins in His own blood." Four months following this sacrifice of lifetime savings Judson and his colleague, Johnathan Wade, burdened by the pressing needs of the field wrote to the secretary of the American Baptist Board of Foreign Missions offering one-twentieth of their allowance and suggested that a similar proposal be made to the Baptist ministers in the United States. Judson and Wade promised that as soon as one hundred ministers made this pledge to transmit to the treasurer one-twentieth of their regular income they would in turn add a second twentieth, thus giving one-tenth to the cause of Baptist missionary endeavor. Within less than a year Judson proposed to reduce his salary by an additional one-fourth, his "mode of living" enabling him to do so, with the stipulation that the arrangement should not interfere with the previous proposals for devotion. News of this action as well as the consecration of Carey and his associates when published in America gave stimulus to the cause of stewardship.

George A. E. Salstrand

10.   SHEEP AND "LAMBS"

"Yes, sir," panted the new sheep herder, "I got in all the sheep, but I had to run some to get those lambs."

"Lambs!" exclaimed the sheep owner, "I have no lambs. Let's see what you got." Looking into the shed, the astonished owner saw fourteen panting jack rabbits! It is just as strenuous a job, and not one whit less difficult, to get men into the sheepfold in the matter of the Separated Portion. We, who are concerned to have men enter the rich fellowship of this partnership with God, must not let the difficulties daunt us or our failures balk us.

Guy L. Morrill

11.   COMING TODAY

Not long ago I read about an estate whose beautiful acreage was expertly tended by a caretaker. Every tree was trimmed, the grass cut, and stately beds of flowers were in bloom. Yet not a soul was around to take in the beauty except the caretaker. A visitor came up to ask, "When was the owner last here?"

"Twelve years ago."

"Then from whom do you get your instructions?"

"From his agent living in Milan."

"But does he ever visit the estate to inspect it?"

"No."

"And yet you keep it trim as if he would come tomorrow?"

The gardener interrupted the curious visitor to say, "As if he were going to come today, sir."

Reuben K. Youngdahl

GIVING

UNDER AUTHORITY

Robert Wilder, founder of the Student Volunteer Movement, sat one day in a hotel in Poona, India. A naval officer with whom he was talking finally said, "Why don't you missionaries stay at home and mind your own business?"

At the time the British fleet had been ordered to Constantinople because of the serious Armenian massacres. Wilder faced the officer, and said:

"Suppose you were ordered to take your battleships to Constantinople tomorrow, and I would say, 'Why don't you stay here and mind your business? There is no sense in your going to the Bosporus.'"

The officer, his dark eyes flashing, retorted, "I would tell you to mind your business. When we are ordered to go, we must go, even if every ship is sunk and every sailor killed."

Wilder then rejoined: "You are right. I also have marching orders, not from any human government, but from the divine government. My command is to preach the gospel to every living creature. India has one-fifth of the world's population, and the primary question is not what the cost is, but whether I am going to obey the command of my Saviour and Lord."

The Christian steward's marching orders are, *The Entire World*; and, at whatever cost of time, money, prayer, life, Christians must carry on until the whole world has heard the glad story of redemption.

Basil Miller

13.   MYSELF

Years ago in the First Baptist Church of Richmond, Virginia, a collection was taken following a missionary address. In one of the plates was a card. The pastor picked it up and found written on it, "Myself. John Lewis Shuck." That was the start of this young man's missionary career. He became the first Baptist missionary appointed to China, sailing for Hong Kong in 1835. If you would be God's steward you must give yourself.

M. *Lunn*

14.   THE PIG AND THE HEN

Philanthropoids have a relevant story. A pig and a hen were strolling amicably down the street when they saw a sign at a lunchroom window reading: DELICIOUS HAM AND EGGS. "Isn't it grand," said the hen, "that together we can give human beings something that delights them?" The pig frowned. "Yes," he said, "but you're giving out of surplus; for me, giving is a real sacrifice."

F. Emerson Andrews

15.   CALVIN ON STEWARDSHIP

To all this we must add a further striking aspect of Calvin's
teaching on the Christian life: his concept of *stewardship*.
Man's possessions are "free gifts of God," and their use may be
summed up in one simple rule, *always prefer the good of others
to our own*. We cannot enrich God with our possessions, but
rather "the saints in the earth": the "sanctified use" of our
goods is the assistance of our neighbour. The Christian is
"debtor to his neighbour," with no bounds fixed to "the exercise
of his beneficence."

> Let this, then, be our rule for benignity and beneficence, that
> whatever God has conferred on us, which enables us to assist
> our neighbour, we are the stewards of it, and must one day
> render an account of our stewardship; and that the only right
> dispensation of what has been committed to us, is that which
> is regulated by the law of love. (Inst 3.7.5)

Joseph C. McLelland

16.   GETTING TREASURES IN HEAVEN

In his presidential address at the Southern Baptist Convention in Miami, Florida, Pat Neff, a layman, said: "All my life
I have heard preachers tell their congregations to lay up treasures in heaven, but none has ever told me how to get my
treasures into heaven. I had to figure it out for myself. The only
way to get our treasures into heaven is to put them into something that is going to heaven. Cattle, lands, houses, stocks and
bonds, oil, coal, and the like are not going to heaven. Only men,
women, boys, and girls are going to heaven. Therefore, if I am
to lay up my treasures in heaven, I must put them to work in

the mighty task of redeeming souls that will be fit for heaven."
That is stewardship in its very essence!

Herschel H. Hobbs

17. THERE IS A LAD HERE

The whole world thrilled to the story of Robert Hill, some
years ago. This thirteen-year-old boy, hearing about the work
of Albert Schweitzer, decided to help by sending a bottle of
aspirin to the good doctor's hospital in Africa. Since his father
was in the Army, stationed in Italy, he asked the Commander
of the Air Force to deliver the bottle of aspirin in one of his
planes. A radio commentator reported the incident on his program, with the result that Robert Hill flew into Africa with four
tons of medical supplies valued at thousands of dollars, on
planes provided by the Italian and French governments. When
Dr. Schweitzer saw the boy he said, "I never knew a little child
could do so much for my hospital." Some would say this was a
matter of charity or compassion; but at a deeper level, it was a
matter of stewardship. Here was a lad, very much like that boy
in scriptures who offered a few fishes and loaves, who gave what
he could in service to others.

Submitted by *Paul Strauch*

18. MODERN MACEDONIANS

In a seminar on Christian social ethics we were discussing
the use of money when Dr. Otto A. Piper, then a professor at
Princeton Theological Seminary, told us this incident from his

post-war work of collecting funds for the relief of the needy in German universities.

Dr. Piper described to a group of Princeton students the conditions of abject poverty in which German students were struggling and asked his hearers to do what they could to help. The next morning a young married couple, both graduate students, came into Dr. Piper's office, placed three hundred dollars on his desk and said, "We heard your talk last night. We have talked it over, and this is our answer to your appeal." He was astonished at the generosity of the gift and said, "Are you sure you can afford this much?" They replied, "It is true that our resources are quite limited. We had saved this money to buy some things that we need. We could use a new refrigerator, and the old car is getting to the point where it should be traded in for a new one. But after all, God has been good to us and we can get along. Those people in Germany need this money much more than we do. We would rather have the joy of giving it to them."

Like Paul's Macedonians (2 Cor. 8:3-4) these young Christians begged for the privilege of giving beyond their means.

T. A. Kantonen

19.   MY LIFE I GIVE

Harry B. McCormick, former president of the United Christian Missionary Society, told of an experience in one of his early pastorates. He happened to be standing by as the officers of the congregation opened the envelopes given in a special missionary offering. All were surprised to find that the largest gift was from a single woman who was the sole support of an invalid mother. The elders said, "This woman cannot afford to give this much."

Dr. McCormick took her check and went to talk with her about it. He explained that she had given more than she could afford, and that the church could not accept it.

After listening to his statement, the woman explained, "My daily work is hard and dull—especially since, as a girl, I had my heart set on going to a foreign field as a missionary. But then my mother became ill, and I had to go to work to support her. I am glad to be able to provide and care for her. But the thing that gives real meaning to my working hours is the thought that I am able, by my giving, to help somebody else go overseas and serve as a missionary. You cannot take away from me this one great joy of my life by refusing to accept my check."

Dr. McCormick says that he went away humbled and chastened. Never again did he attempt to tell anybody that he was giving too much to Christ.

Harold L. Lunger

20. TRANSLATING DOLLARS

I was in southeastern Nebraska, "setting up" in a number of the churches what has come to be known widely as the New Financial Plan. One evening I held a group meeting in a village church, where most of the officers were retired farmers. I presented the plan, and made it clear from charts and diagrams— the every-member canvass, the weekly offering, the "duplex" envelope, in a word, intelligent business methods in the finances of the church. But the men did not respond. I spoke again, showing the record of other village churches where the plan had been tried, and seeking to make it plain that such methods, if adopted, would certainly double the financial income, and greatly increase the efficiency of their own church. Still there was no response, and I asked a shrewd looking farmer sitting near the stove if I had made the matter clear.

He leaned forward and pointed a long index finger at charts: "They's a ketch in it," he said.

"Why, my brother, I intended to make it very plain."

"O, it's plain enough," and the shrewd eyes half closed as he continued, "but they's a ketch in it all the same; they's deceit in it; for I can see, if we adopt this plan, we'll be payin' out more money then we intend to give."

Harvey Reeves Calkins

21.   DOES YOUR GIFT REPRESENT YOU?

It happened one time after a pastor had made an appeal in church for a great and worthy cause, that a certain woman, a member of the church, came to him and handed him a check for $50, asking at the same time if her gift was satisfactory. The pastor immediately replied, "If it represents you." There was a moment of soul searching thought and she asked to have the check returned to her. She left with it and a day or two later she returned handing the pastor a check for $5,000 and again asking the same question, "Is my gift satisfactory?" The pastor gave the same answer as before, "If it represents you." As before, a truth seemed to be driving deeply. After a few moments of hesitation she took back the check and left. Later in the week she came again with a check. That time it was for $50,000. As she placed it in the pastor's hand she said, "After earnest, prayerful thought I have come to the conclusion that this gift does represent me and I am happy to give it." Perhaps in this light the words from I Corinthians 16:2 "as God hath prospered him," may take on new meaning.

John Allan Lavendar

22.   PROPORTIONATE GIVING

At a church service in Paris many years ago an offering was being received for foreign missions. A poor blind woman placed 27 francs on the offering plate. A friend sitting beside her whispered, "Surely you are making a mistake, for you cannot afford to give that much." "Oh yes, I can," she replied, "I can well afford it." Later she gave this explanation of her apparently extravagant giving. "I am blind," she said, "and so I asked my fellow-workers in basket weaving how much they spent a year in order to do additional work in the evenings. They came up with the sum of 27 francs. That is then the amount which I have saved this year, for I am blind and do not need light as I work. I am therefore in a position to give this amount for bringing the light of truth into the darkness of the heathen."

Here is also new light on proportionate giving.

SANA, *Helsinki, Finland*

23.   THERE IS A GIRL HERE

"Master, there is a girl here"—born of a Christian bonds-woman and an Irish chieftain, churning butter in her father's pantry over sixteen hundred years ago. Vivid and energetic and generous, she would make twelve ordinary pats of butter and a larger thirteenth one to give the passing stranger, for the sake of the Saviour; not to mention twelve loaves of bread, plus a larger thirteenth loaf. She had a little song for singing as she churned or baked:

O God, bless my pantry!
Pantry which the Lord has blessed, never be lacking in aught.
O Mary's Son, my Friend, come and come into my pantry,
Let there be abundance ever on the board for Thee.

Thousands of Irish peasant girls and princesses came under St. Bridget's teaching; and across these sixteen centuries clergymen of her church still cherish the prayer she made at one of their early training conferences:

I would like the angels of heaven to be among us.
I would like full baskets for charity.
I would like rich treasures of mercy.
I would like cheerfulness to reign over us all.
I would like Jesus to be present.
I would like the three Marys of the gospel to be with us.
I would like myself to be a rent-payer to the Lord.

Margaret T. Applegarth

24.   I NEVER PLEDGE

"I never sign a pledge of any kind," said a man whom I was soliciting.

"Are you sure?" I asked.

"Yes," he replied.

"Do you own your home?" I questioned.

"Yes, but it is mortgaged for half its value."

"Did you promise to pay interest on your mortgage?"

"Yes."

"When your telephone was installed, did you agree to pay monthly charges?"

"Yes. What are you driving at?"

"As a matter of fact," I answered, "have you not committed the larger portion of your income to everything your home needs except the church?"

"I surrender," he said.

Robert Cashman

25.   PART OF THE GIFT

As for *feet,* Mr. Standfast in *Pilgrim's Progress* painted the
perfect picture: "I have loved to hear my Lord spoken of; and
wherever I have seen the print of His shoe in the earth, there
I have been delighted to place mine also." It means the stewardship of the second mile; or the third; or the fourth. Even
up to the eighth—for rather recently an Indian woman crossed
her entire reservation, carrying a pottery vase she had made as
a good-by gift for the missionary going on furlough. As he
traced the exquisite old tribal patterns, he said gratefully: "And
to think that you walked eight miles to bring it to me, and will
have the same eight miles back!" Her brown face showed surprise: *"But the walk is part of the gift,"* she explained to show
that she had known all along what a vase involved. ("How
beautiful are the feet of them that bring glad tidings, and pub-
lish peace.") No shoe store in town can furnish a new You with
this tirelessness: it is part of an unpayable debt and a lavish
overglow of goodwill.

                                        Margaret T. Applegarth

26.   THE VALLEY OF THE NILE

Across northern Africa stretches the largest desert in the
world. Yet at its eastern edge is one of the richest and most
fertile valleys known to man.

The valley of the Nile is not fertile simply because a river
flows through it: It is fertile because that river *overflows,*
depositing each year another layer of tropical soil washed down
from the jungles of central Africa.

The mere flow of our lives is meaningless in the desert world. But the man whose life overflows makes the life of his Church as fruitful as the valley of the Nile.

Henry B. Luffberry

27.   THE SACRIFICE OF LOVE

It was a great privilege to preach in the Christian church in Lotumbe, where I was the house guest of Dr. and Mrs. John Ross. I was alerted to the possibility of a visit from members of the church. Sure enough, following the etiquette of African custom, about midmorning of the following day, a delegation of some twenty or twenty-five members of the congregation came to the Ross home. They sang a hymn, thanked God for my visit, and prayed for my safe return. Then the spokesman of the group presented me with thirty francs, about sixty cents. I was inarticulate. Later I was told that it took these dear people about half a day to raise thirty francs, in fact they had begun on Sunday afternoon. I was humbled and overcome as I realized there are people in the world who are that poor—yet that dedicated.

We glibly quote statistics from the United Nations, advising us that four out of five people have never had a square meal in their lives and probably never will have, that four out of five people in the world have never seen a competent physician and probably never will, but not until we move among such people in various parts of the world do the statistics take on visible bodies and faces.

I shall never spend that thirty francs. I shall keep the gift to remind me of a people who sacrificed to lavish love on a stranger. This gift is recorded in my heart as the largest and most appreciated honorarium I have ever received.

Jack V. Reeve

28.   "IN THE PENCIL"

Teacher (to a little girl learning to write): "But where is the dot over the 'i'?"

Little Girl: "It's in the pencil yet."

Many people let their good intentions stay in their hearts and their intended philanthropies stay in their pockets. We must put the dot over the "i." We must get out the vote. We must sign men up in the fellowship of stewardship.

Guy L. Morrill

GRACE

29.   Love So Amazing

Little John is an incorrigible child, swept by storms of selfish temper. He seems to be incapable of love to anyone. His parents can do nothing with him. But so far as his selfish little heart knows love at all, it is directed towards Tim, his wire-haired terrier. He has been teaching the dog a trick. The dog is slow to learn, and John in a temper kicks it in the mouth. The little dog, with its tongue red with its own blood, licks its master's hand. John, who has taken innumerable "lickings" unmoved, cannot take this one. He runs indoors to his mother, and cries out, "Mummy, I've been a bad boy."

The Cross shows what happened when "God so loved the world that He gave his only-begotten Son." He gave what was most precious to Him, that He might win the people of the world. What a standard Christ sets His followers!

Lindsay Dewar

21

30.   FIVE GRAINS OF CORN

In early New England it was the custom at Thanksgiving to place five grains of corn at every plate as a reminder of the first winter, when food was so depleted that only five grains of corn were rationed to each individual at a time. The Pilgrim Fathers wanted their children to remember the suffering which made possible the settlement of a free people in a free land, that on the day in which their ration was so reduced only seven healthy colonists remained to nurse the sick and nearly half their numbers lay in the "windswept graveyard" on the hill, but when the Mayflower sailed back to England, only the sailors were aboard. Perhaps it would help us to be more grateful if we see five grains of corn beside our Thanksgiving plates.

Letter to Members
The Lutheran Church, Missouri Synod.

31.   GRATITUDE

Dr. Albert Palmer, at one time pastor of the Central Union Church in Honolulu, one day opened the door of his study to find standing there a Japanese man almost completely hidden by an enormous bunch of chrysanthemums. He entered the study with many bows, and then said, "You speak so nice about my people, I bring you these." What Dr. Palmer had done was to write a letter to one of the newspapers defending the Japanese against some unwarranted attack, and voicing his appreciation of them and his confidence in them. This little man had read the letter in his home in Hilo, on another island nearly

200 miles away, and had come over to Honolulu to say "thank you" in characteristic Japanese fashion.

Albert J. Penner

32. THE TOP FOUR INCHES

Dr. A. E. Morgan, one of the first of the administrators of the Tennessee Valley Authority and a great scientist, was accustomed to explain the philosophy of soil, power, and wealth in terms of the gifts of God. As a Christian he saw an amazing balance of powers in the "top four inches of the earth's crust" which was designed to feed men for all time. "But you must remember," he would say, "that we do not create any of it. We only learn to use it as God has created it."

Roy L. Smith

33. NOT AS THE WORLD GIVES

The great gift, the unique and living one, is not a thing but a person. It is Jesus Christ himself. In him God has given himself, no longer just things which he creates or has created, but his own person, his own suffering, and his own solitude, given unto death itself. He declared it himself, just before turning to face his cross: "Greater love has no man than this, that a man lay down his life for his friend." This gift of all gifts is the self-commitment of God himself, who carried it through to the bitter end so that we may entrust ourselves to it.

The almost unbelievable news of the revelation is that it really is a gift. It is free, without reservation and without recall. Whatever our virtues may be, whatever may be our times of repentance, they all would be unequal to the payment of such a treasure. Thus it is that God offers it freely. He is the One who has paid its price, in the death of his Son. The erasure of all our failings and all our remorse, of all our regrets and our rebellion, what a gift it is! The redemption of all our joys about to be swallowed up in death, and their fulfillment in eternal joy itself—what a gift indeed!

Paul Tournier

MONEY

34.

The publishing firm of Holt, Rinehart and Winston gave poet Robert Frost 18 shares of stock in January 1929. He lost them. After his death, his executor found the original certificate in a trunk in the poet's home in an envelope postmarked "January 2, 1929."

In 1931, these 18 shares had a market value of $67.50. Through stock dividends and splits the shares had grown to 933 with a market value of over $28,000 by 1963.

from The Christian Will

35. MONEY

Dug from the mountain side, washed in the glen,
Servant am I or the master of men
   Steal me, I curse you,

Earn me, I bless you;
Grasp me and hoard me, a fiend shall possess you;
Lie for me, die for me;
Covet me, take me,
Angel or devil, I am what you make me.

Author Unknown

36.   THE BIGGEST KICK

When the noted editor William Allen White gave the city
of Emporia fifty acres of land for a public park, he said as he
gave the deed to the mayor, "This is the last kick in a fistful of
dollars that I am giving away today. I have always tried to teach
that there are three kicks in every dollar: one when you make it,
another when you save it, the third when you give it . . . I get
the biggest kick of all in this last one."

Milo Kauffman

37.   WHAT IS A DOLLAR?

Take a silver dollar. Place it in the hand of a chemist and
ask him to tell you what it contains. He will presently report
to you that the coin is made up of "metal," which, on being dissolved at the laboratory, is found to contain silver, lead, and
zinc, besides a small residuum of phosphates and tin. Apparently, this exhausts the contents of the coin, for the chemist
says there is nothing more in it. But there is another test. Place
the coin in the hand of a poor widow and ask her to tell you

what it contains. To-morrow she will report that it is made up of "values," which on being dissolved or released at the store, are found to contain meat, fruit, and vegetables, together with a very large supply of consolation and hope. Value as well as metal was stored in that minted coin, but the former could not be released in the laboratory of the chemist. The fine spiritual force of money can be reached only by the mind and spirit of a man. It can be released and set to work only in the wide laboratory of human society.

Harvey Reeves Calkins

38.   MONEY HAS POWER

We say "money talks" but we also know that money can make people quiet. It has power to secure or defeat justice, to make or break life, to make clear or muddy the stream of life, and it can promote or retard the kingdom of God.

Ben Hagelbarger

39.   GOD'S GOLD

Who can ever forget the story of Achan, one of Joshua's men who kept "devoted things" under his tent because of selfishness. At a time when everything pointed to a great victory, tragic defeat gave Israel a shocking setback. When Joshua rent his clothes and asked God the reason for this, the Lord said, "Israel has sinned." Then it was discovered that Achan, contrary to the will of God, had hid a beautiful mantle, 200 shekels of silver, and 50 shekels of gold under his tent. He had claimed for himself that which had been devoted to God.

A. *Dale Fiers*

40.   THE POT OF INCOME

A little girl who had been left to watch the soup was presently heard to call out: "O Mother, come quick. The soup is getting bigger than the pot." How can the life of the home be spiritual-minded when the family's expenditures are forever getting bigger than their pot of income so that debt and anxiety and worry and indifference and carelessness and loss of confidence and self-respect prevail? Peace and hope and assurance and joy have no place in such a home.

Guy L. Morrill

41.   DISTURBING AMERICAN PORTRAIT

Recently a research organization announced that the cash lost in the United States annually amounts to about $75 per person. That amount is greater than the per member contributions in the median range of twenty-three church bodies. The word "lost" was used literally, that is, money that falls out of pockets or that is in wallets or purses which are misplaced, etc. Only the Lord knows what the amount would be if the statement had included money that disappeared through bad luck in business investments or bingo or poker or the horses.

Commenting on this announcement in the *Saturday Review*, Norman Cousins wrote:

Completely unrelated but not irrelevant is another vital statistic. The total average income for most of the human occupants of this planet comes to about $69 per person. *In short, the average American misplaces more money each year than almost anyone else receives* . . . There is something damnably itchy about these prickly statistics. You feel like scratching, but don't quite know where to find the bite. It is like wearing unlined tweed next to the skin; the better the tweed the more uncomfortable it gets . . . Whatever one does or does not do about the jabbing statistics, one thing at least is clear. They don't lend themselves to adjustment. No philosophical formulation, be it ever so sophisticated, can possibly provide the accommodating ointment . . . *What do we do? Perhaps we had better go on scratching—at least until we find the bite.* (Saturday Review, July 28, 1962, p. 29: italics added.)

Arthur R. McKay

42. "Down Payment" in the New Testament

The way in which certain words were used in the Greek papyri has served to illumine their meaning in the New Testament writings. Thus the term "earnest" was commonly employed in *koine* Greek to describe a down payment, as a preliminary to the balance being discharged in full at a subsequent time. One papyrus stipulated that certain dancing-girls engaged for a village festival were to receive some money as an advance payment of their salary, where the word "earnest" was used in precisely the New Testament sense of an advance bestowal of what will be fully completed later on.

In those papyri which recorded commercial dealings, the word for "seal" commonly occurred, either to describe a silver seal, a signet ring, or a seal impression. As a verb it was employed in the technical sense of sealing up bags of wheat and barley in order to make proper delivery. It was against such a background and with such a precise usage in view that St. Paul, in writing to the church in Rome, informed the believers that all the appropriate steps regarding the collection for the poor in Jerusalem had been taken, and that he, like an honest merchant, would see to it that the delivery was properly effected. Of the many examples which it is possible to cite, the foregoing will serve to indicate the way in which the popular idiom was consistently adapted and transformed by the New Testament writers in order to describe some new spiritual experience or dimension.

R. K. Harrison

43.   MONEY CHANGERS IN THE TEMPLE

This phrase, taken from the act of our Lord recorded in Matt. 21:12, is usually taken to describe something deplorable, the sordid, the profaning of religion by commercialism. But in the highest sense, each Christian can be a "money changer." When a person brings money to be used in furthering the program and purposes of Christ, money becomes changed into life. Money can be changed into health and life in a hospital down the street or across the sea; it can be changed into a college where a young person finds what is needful for real living. It is changed into food as the Church meets physical need in all parts of the earth. By its right use, money is the alchemy by which human life and energy are transported from one place to another. Hence, "the offering of an upright man enriches the altar, and its fragrance reaches the Most High" (Ecclesiasticus 35:5-6).

By our money we can talk in many languages to proclaim the gospel; by our money we can heal the sick, give sight to the blind, care for the fatherless, teach the ignorant and feed the hungry. Hence it becomes the "open sesame" to a glorious ministry.

You—yes, you—can be a money changer in the temple!

Gordon W. Mattice

44. THE ROAD GOD TRAVELS

It is through the physical that God reveals Himself to us. "First the natural and then the spiritual" (I Cor. 15:46) is Paul's declaration to the Christians at Corinth. God lays the roads from Himself to us in the natural or physical. He descends to us and we ascend to Him through the senses of our nature and the material elements of life.

This truth was made vivid to me shortly after I came to Richmond when one evening I went to hear our symphony orchestra, conducted by the brilliant Edgar Schenkman. The principal composition of the program was Dvorak's Symphony V in E Minor. It was an aesthetic and spiritual experience to me. How did it come? Through the physical, of course. It could not have been received any other way.

Schenkman is a vital physical anatomy of one hundred seventy-five pounds. The baton with which he conducted was ebony; the hand that held it was skin, bone, sinew, and muscle. The players were solid persons, even as you and I. The musical scores on the paper were physical notes, written and drawn between physical lines. The instruments were of wood, brass, silver, and gut. The music which came forth was a succession of coordinated, blended, and toned physical vibrations, but by it I was transported from my work-a-day world and its problems and responsibilities to higher realms. Ecstasy, with its pain and pleasure, emotion and aspiration, laid hold on me. It was a genuine spiritual experience, coming through the physical. Some foolish people speak scornfully of money. A mere piece of paper, a bit of metal, they say. But without "hard cash," how many churches, schools, colleges, seminaries, hospitals, remedial and creative agencies would there be, bringing spiritual, cultural, healing, and recreational values to America and the world? First the natural and then the physical.

I thank God for money; I make no apologies about asking for it, and rejoice in those who give as unto the Lord.

James W. Clarke

45.   CHILDREN WITHOUT ADVANTAGES

Not long ago a magazine told the story of a Methodist preacher who lived in London on a salary of seven hundred and fifty dollars a year. He had a wife and five daughters. Bringing up five daughters on seven hundred and fifty dollars a year would not seem to allow for many material advantages. If circumstances were similar to those of other homes maintained on such a salary, the busy mother doubtless had cooking and dishwashing, cleaning, mending, and sewing to do. More than likely the children had to help with the dishes and the dusting and get their lessons by themselves. But these girls grew up. Four of the five married. The first became Lady Edward Burne-Jones, wife of the great artist. The second became Lady Edward Poynter, wife of the president of the Royal Academy and mother of Sir Hugh Poynter, one of the big steel men of Canada. The third married John Kipling and became the mother of Rudyard Kipling. The fourth married a man named Baldwin. Her son, Stanley, is a former prime minister of England. Poor little girls! It was too bad that they could not have had "advantages."

Guy L. Morrill

46. A Month's Wages

The Rev. J. Ross Stevenson, when pastor of the Fifth Avenue Presbyterian Church, New York City, received a letter enclosing a month's wages from a Swedish servant girl, just before the annual offering for foreign missions was to be taken. She wrote that she had been making the offering a subject of special prayer and it had been put into her heart to give this sum. Lest Satan should tempt her not to give so much, if she waited until Sunday, she sent it at once. When the pastor read the note from the pulpit, there was a profound silence, and the offering that day was doubled by the example of one girl's sacrifice.

Two men who had come over from New Jersey for that service walked down the avenue afterward together without either saying a word for some distance. One asked the other whether he could lend him money to get home; then his friend confessed that he, too, had put into the offering every cent he had with him. Both were obliged to walk to the ferry and find a good samaritan in Jersey City to assist them to get home.

David McConaughy

PRACTICE

47.   SAY IT!

Many of us admire the strong, silent type of person for whom
Vermont has become famous. But I think it was rather too
long silence which the Vermont farmer broke, when he said to
his wife as he sat whittling on the porch, "Do you know, Sarah,
you have meant so much to me that sometimes it's almost more
than I can stand not to tell you about it." Most of us go too
long without telling those nearest to us how much they mean
to us. Silence is golden but it can become leaden. So is it in
our relations with God. We become more responsive to God's
goodness by expressing our response.

Ralph W. Sockman

48.   SERVE WHERE YOU ARE

A policeman in Birmingham on becoming a Christian was
so greatly troubled by the sights and sounds of sin among

which he worked that for a long time he prayed, "Lord, take me out of the police service. Give me some other work."

Still no answer came and no other work was opened to him. At last he said to his wife: "I think we have been making a great mistake. We have been praying that I may be taken out of the force, and I begin to think that He has put me there to work. Now I am going to pray that He will help me to serve where I am."

That was the beginning of a life of marvelous usefulness. His influence over the men was so great that he was promoted to be the head of the detectives. He was instrumental in the salvation of many criminals. The place where God has put you is the place where you can do the best service for Him.

M. Lunn

49.   OTHER MEN'S GRIEF

An old druggist from Springfield, Illinois, made the journey to Washington on one occasion for no other purpose than to see Abraham Lincoln and "tell him a few yarns." It had been Mr. Lincoln's habit to stop in at the drug store from time to time to exchange stories with the quaint old man, and one day the druggist discovered that he usually did it when he was on the eve of a difficult law case, or when he had some special load on his mind.

The old apothecary was under no delusions as to his own skill as a politician, and he had no requests to make of the president nor suggestions as to how the war was to be conducted. But he did have some good stories that were designed to relieve anxiety, and armed with a mind full of fun and good cheer he presented himself at the White House and was given a cordial welcome.

Late that night, when the dinner was done and all the guests were gone, Mr. Lincoln and Uncle Billy found themselves alone in a quiet place. It was then that the President said, "Billy, what did you come to Washington for?"

"Just to see you, Mr. Lincoln," the old druggist replied. "Just to see you and tell you some yarns."

"Didn't you want a post office, or anything?" the President persisted.

"No sir. I just wanted to be with you for a little while."

And with that the President bowed his head for a moment, and lifting his eyes, infinitely sad, he began to unload his heart. For an hour he poured out into the ear of the man he could trust all the pain and grief of his soul. No one knows what the Union may owe to the humble man who assumed a stewardship over another man's grief in the hour of his testing.

Roy L. Smith

50.   SMALL BEGINNINGS

In Alexandria, Louisiana, is one of the most beautiful church auditoriums in the South. For years the church worshiped in an inadequate educational building. The adult membership spoke of the need for a place of worship, but always they spoke of debt and of the large sum of money involved. Finally, after about fifteen years, a miracle happened. One Sunday night Miss Lena Davis talked to her Intermediate Training Union about the need for an auditorium costing many thousands of dollars. At the close of her remarks someone suggested that they take up an offering with which to start a building fund. They did, and received something like $3.56. This was turned over to the pastor, who announced the sum in the church bulletin as the beginning of a building fund. A bank president in the congregation saw the article, and mailed a sizable check to the church. Others caught the challenge, and today there stands on the corner of Fourth and Jackson "the church in the heart of the city, in the heart of the state, for the hearts of the people." But nearest and dearest to the heart of God was that first gift to build a monument to him—and to the daring consecration of youth.

Herschel H. Hobbs

51.   SMALL UNITS

Franz Kafka's account of the building of the Great Wall of China is a suggestive allegory. He recounts that this great wall was constructed in small units; otherwise, the gigantic task would have exceeded the hope and imagination of the builders. Shih Huang reputedly erected one-half the 1500-mile long wall during his 36-year rule. Men of a given village were conscripted to erect a limited, compassable portion. They went to their task in parade form, with banners flying, and to the blare of trumpets. They were welcomed home as a triumphal army which had won a victory. They had accomplished the assigned task, even though much was left to be done.

Stewardship development is a never ending task, for Christ's battle for God's world is a never ceasing warfare.

Winburn T. Thomas

52.   FAITHFUL IN LITTLE, FAITHFUL IN MUCH

Anxious as he had been at seventeen and eighteen to save capital for establishing himself in business, John D. Rockefeller had not failed to give generously to church and charity. The most creditable chapter in the young man's life is that recorded in the pages of his first account book, the "Ledger A" which he began in 1855. Entries from December 1855, to April 1956, show that he had received less than $95 for four months' work. Out of this he had paid $1 for pew-rent in the Erie Street Church, a small sum for a religious paper, and $5.88 for various charitable objects. His gifts for the four months just about balanced the sum he spent for clothing, $9.09. This was a remarkable performance: On his meagre income, allowing himself almost nothing for amusements, and skimping on luncheons, he had approached a literal interpretation of the Biblical injunction respecting a tithe of man's earnings.

And he gave more than money; he gave time and labor. The Erie Street Church was a poor man's conventicle, in a rapidly growing part of town populated mainly by clerks, artisans, and shopkeepers. It had a poor, uncarpeted, ill-lighted auditorium and a badly paid minister. Rockefeller served as clerk to the church, paying the costs for postage and stationery, and after a time as Sunday School teacher.

Allan Nevins

53.   DISCIPLINE COMES FIRST

Spontaneous generosity doesn't always come forth at the time of great need or appeal. Discipline is the basis of most action which may result in joyous experience. And discipline must usually come first. This makes discipline a priority rather than spontaneity and, of course, there is a very practical limitation to the principle of spontaneity, namely, that the income may have all been spent before the appeal comes or the generous impulse is felt.

Edwin A. Briggs

54.   INTEREST THROUGH EXPERIENCE

Our local churches must look to this task of preserving the personal element. It is more difficult to maintain the same per capita interest in a church of two thousand members than in a church of two hundred members. The tendency in large parishes is to substitute organization for individual effort and responsibility. And there is no substitute for personal work in religion. Spiritual vitality is maintained by individual practice. In high school I never took much interest in chemistry until I was sent into the laboratory to perform some experiments. I blew up some test tubes and burned my fingers but I caught something of the thrill of chemistry. Similarly in the church, our young people do not get the thrill of religion by merely hearing sermons or listening to teachers in Sunday School classes. We must give them laboratories where they can experiment with the principles of Jesus. Young people drop out of the church at the point where we fail to take them over from the lecture stage to the laboratory stage of religion. And around every church are community laboratories where we can, if we will, try out the teachings of Jesus.

Ralph W. Sockman

55.   WHEN STEWARDSHIP IS QUEENLY

In the early months of World War II the warship on which I was serving put in at Tongatabu, Tonga Islands. This port was outstanding in being the only one in both oceans where we dropped anchor where a sailor could find no woman of the streets to pick up, no place to gamble, no place to get drunk. The Polynesian natives were all Christian, all literate. Most of them were Wesleyan Methodists, and all of them were happy. The sailors were happy, too, when they came back on board.

So was the ship's captain when he had no disciplinary cases at mast the next morning.

Tongatabu has become famous these days for its Queen Salote, a large, handsome, lovable mother devoted to service for her people as a Christian. The story is told that her father, reigning until Salote's middle teens, died quite suddenly without his eldest daughter having been prepared for the shock. When informed that she was catapulted into the queenship, her first question was, "Isn't there anyone else?"

James V. Claypool

56. REVEILLE

The old man was bedfast, victim of a paralytic stroke. His eyes gleamed mistily as we talked of our little church, its rapid growth, its new building. "Pastor," he murmured, "I'd give anything to be able to come to church *one* Sunday, but I know I'll never get out of this bed."

Smiling ruefully he went on, "There was a time when I could have come to church every Sunday—but then I preferred to stay in bed."

It is ironic how our sense of values can change. Fortunate is the man who awakens in time to the worth of worship and work in the house of God.

Henry B. Luffberry

57. TWENTIETH CENTURY SAMARITANS

Anyone who lives through a tornado is likely to remember it for a long time. This was our experience in southern Ontario when we were visited by "Hurricane Hazel." The damage was immense to orchards, buildings, bridges, and anything else that stood in its way. Dazed farmers pondered how long it would be before their property would be back to normal. But early one morning in the London area, busloads of Mennonites began to arrive from farms near Kitchener. With concerted effort they set to work clearing up rubble, building barns, and restoring order. They asked no pay, nor would they accept any. It was, they said, just part of their religion. Many a farmer throughout the area must have pondered on how much the churches have lost by not doing more of this. No one man could take the credit for it. Families who had never set foot inside a Mennonite church were helped on life's way by the spirit of Christ alive in the hearts of other Christians.

Robert Mackie

58.　　　　PooR WithOUT Poverty

It sometimes happens that a godly woman without financial rank in the town contributes more to the actual spiritual power of the congregation than some person of wealth whose life is undedicated, but whose money is liberally bestowed.

"She is the penniless power house of our church," said a certain pastor in speaking of a woman who was rendering an amazing service among the youth of the congregation. In the course of ten years perhaps a hundred youngsters had been utterly transformed through the radiance of her personal life, yet she was never able to give more than a dollar a week to the financial support of the church.

Roy L. Smith

59.   A MODERN PARABLE

A certain nation fell among thieves and that nation was wounded and robbed and stripped of its goods, and left half dead. And by chance there came a sister nation, who referred the matter to the UN Security Council. This wealthy nation also sent a note of protest to the offending nation, and then went its way.

And likewise a second nation, which called itself a Christian nation, came and looked at her, and passed by on the other side. This nation went home and organized a committee to send its worn-out clothing to the wounded nation.

But a third nation had compassion on the suffering of this wounded nation, and opened its borders to the starving, the homeless and the helpless of that wounded land.

Which now of these three, thinkest thou, was neighbor unto that nation which fell among thieves?

Paraphrase by Harvey N. Chinn

60.   LIFE IS A PARTNERSHIP

When the fishing boats return to the harbor, they are often encircled by a flock of sea gulls. Some perch on the boat within an arm's length of the fisherman.

There is a reason why the birds feel so fearless and friendly. The fishermen usually throw their leftover bait and fish waste to the birds. The gulls have learned that a fishing boat means a generous dinner.

The fishermen should feel friendly to the sea gulls, too. Whenever they see the gulls hovering closely over a patch of water, they know there is a school of fish nearby. In the midst of a thick fog sailors can sometimes locate land by listening to the cries of the gulls along the shore.

The fishermen and the sea gulls are partners. They help each other and they depend on each other.

All life is made up of partnerships, and this is especially true of men. We could not live as we do without the material and moral support of many persons. And we in turn must help others. This is more than a cold business arrangement. It is the command of Jesus! "A new commandment I give unto you, that ye love one another . . . By this shall all men know that you are my disciples, if ye have love one to another" (John 13:34-35). Our Lord intended that his love should be expressed through personal concern and active service to others. It is to be an unselfish love!

The Golden Rule is the embodiment of the law and the epitome of love. We have a sacred responsibility to help one another. Life is a partnership!

Rolla O. Swisher

61.   JOY IN A TENEMENT

One bleak Christmas eve a Yale student, spending his vacation in settlement work in the lower end of New York City, found a German widow woman in a cheerless attic tenement with three little daughters down with typhoid fever, without fuel or food or medical attention. He got fuel and made a fire, brought food and a doctor. One of the children died; the other two recovered. The woman came to the Neighborhood House, then to the church, then to Christ. Hearing of the famine in India, she made up her mind to show her gratitude by taking up the support of one or more Indian famine waifs in memory of the little girl whom she had lost. She was earning her living and supporting her family by scrubbing floors at night in a great office building in the neighborhood. Out of her hard-earned wages, she began to set aside a dollar and a half a week, and found that she was able thus to take care of four famine waifs. She also began to interest herself in those about her in the neighborhood who were in poorer circumstances than herself. On the following Christmas eve, when I went to the new rooms to which she had moved from her attic tenement, I found that she had papered them with her own hands and had put in a baby organ, on which the children were learning to play. She gathered together a group of poor children for a Christmas party and got her fellow scrub-women to join in providing for the treat. Out of the new-born love for her Savior, she soon had learned the great lesson of Christian giving.

David McConaughy

62. GOD'S HOUSE

The small Iowa county-seat town was ultra-conservative in both politics and economy. The same basic thought prevailed in the life of the church.

The church building was old and had long since passed its true purpose of providing facilities for the tri-fold needs of the congregation: worship, education and fellowship. Yet the pastor sought in vain to stir the members to give funds for a new structure. Discouraged, and of the opinion that the congregation would gradually die, "crumbling away with the ancient building," the pastor had determined to move when the breakthrough came.

A couple, faithful members who had reached the age of retirement were planning to build a new home. They had carefully saved over the years and the money for the new home was in the bank. They called the pastor to their present home, a modest but well-kept one, and said to him, "We have decided that this house, where we have lived for over forty years, is all right for the rest of our lives. We want the money we have saved for a new house to be used for a greater purpose."

Today there is an adequate church building in this Iowa town. The congregation faces the future rather than lives in the past. All have shared and found joy in their sharing, but they gave only when challenged and inspired by a couple who said: ". . . for a greater purpose."

Julian E. Stuart

63.   BROTHERS ALL

Back in the years when the Jews were undergoing horrors at the hands of Hitler, a young preacher put up a great sign on the corner of his church which read: "This church is joining with other Christians in prayer in behalf of the persecuted Jews of Europe."

Because the church stood alongside a much travelled boulevard, the sign was read by tens of thousands of people every week. From a considerable number of Jewish citizens there came phone calls of deep appreciation. Many months later the pastor was surprised one day to have the rabbi of one of the leading synagogues of the city appear at his study, asking for "a little time to talk over some personal matters." No reference was made to the sign, but the rabbi produced some European letters which told of terrors, murders, starvation, hunger, deaths, and long night vigils of prayer. They had come from brothers and sisters of the rabbi, in several cities of the continent.

"Why have you come to me with this?" the preacher asked the rabbi finally.

"Because I have to preach to my congregation tonight," the rabbi answered, "and practically every family among my people will be carrying other letters like these. I am heartsick and I have no word within me for them. But I know you have been praying for my people and I thought I could come to you, and perhaps you could give me some word of hope and courage that I might pass on to Israel."

For more than an hour the two men of God talked together and before they parted they joined in prayer. "I will tell my people tonight," the rabbi said as he started to leave, "that I have heard a Christian clergyman pray for us, and that will make them a little braver."

The following Sunday morning, just before he entered the pulpit, the preacher received a telephone call. It was from the rabbi. "I wanted you to get the word before you went into your pulpit," he said. "Last Friday night I preached and comforted my people. I told them we had prayed together, and that I had heard you pray for Israel, and they asked me to get this word to you. They entered into a solemn covenant that at eleven o'clock this morning, when you are preaching to your people, three hundred and fifty Jewish families in this city will be in prayer in your behalf."

No preacher ever went into his pulpit with more of a sense of holy awe upon him than that morning when that preacher entered his, and began to preach.

Roy L. Smith

64. FIRST CENTURY BOARD MEETING

The men were in a huddle. "Fellows," one of them was saying, "we've just got to do something about it. . . . We can't have any more embarrassing situations like that one this afternoon. All those hungry people out there wanting bread, and us with no dough. . . ."

Andy nodded. "Yeah, we were sure lucky that guy with the

bag lunch turned up. But we can't expect to be bailed out by a miracle every time we don't have any money. . . ."

"Now that you've brought the matter up," said Bart, "you don't know how embarrassed I've been about our financial situation. We've had a rough time making ends meet ever since we got started. What we really need around here are some good moneymaking projects. Something that will draw a lot of people and be the occasion for some real good old-fashioned Christian fellowship. . . .

"The trouble today is that people just don't get together like they used to. Now the other day, when we were over at Mary and Martha's house . . . remember that lamb stew Martha fixed for us?"

The group murmured appreciatively. "And that fried fish Pete's mother-in-law served us in Capernaum last week?"

The group murmured again. "Why don't we get the women organized and then put on some fish fries in Capernaum and maybe a couple of lamb suppers in Bethany? That ought to help out our treasury—and also advance the kingdom."

"Better still," said Matt, "how about setting up some bazaars and auctions? One thing my experience in the financial world taught me is that the time-tested approaches to the market are the best. A rummage sale would be good, too—especially the way people throw away their garments every time a visiting fireman enters the city."

"The important thing," said Jim, "is to set up projects that involve as many people as possible. Involvement—that's the key word. If we don't give them something to do, they'll start drifting away. For instance, how about a mail-order service offering honey-covered locusts?

"We could ask one of the ladies' societies to take this on as a special stewardship project. They could roast the locusts, dip them in honey, and then package them for wholesale delivery by camel caravan to every local group in the country. Then each group could sell the boxes at retail prices and pocket the profit. Hopefully a portion of this would then be sent in to us for our work. We could even give each group a free urn for a certain number of boxes sold."

"And where would we get the urns?" asked Tom doubtfully. His question was lost in the shuffle.

"While we're at it," Phil said, "let's not forget the kids. We ought to give them something to do, too. They could sponsor a donkey wash on weekends and maybe do some gleaning out in the fields on a special work day. Don't forget they're the future church."

"You know," said Judas, "this has been one of the best sessions we've had since we organized. At last I feel that we're moving . . ."

Theodore A. Braun

65.   GOD'S INSTRUMENT

Not many sermons which we hear in childhood are clearly remembered in later life. One which I heard as a boy, however, made such a deep impression upon me that I have never forgotten it. It centered upon an interpretation of Psalm 92:3, an exhortation to praise God "upon an instrument of ten strings." Upon becoming a theological student I discovered that my pastor had been guilty of "forced exegesis." Nor could he lay any claim to originality, for I have encountered the same line of thought in various other settings. Yet this quaint interpretation which was evidently quite popular a half-century ago carries a stewardship message which is permanently valid.

"What is this instrument of ten strings?" asked the preacher. And he answered, "It is you. You have two eyes to see what God has done. You have two ears to hear God's word. You have two hands to do God's work. You have two feet to walk God's way. You have one tongue to speak God's truth. You have one heart to give to God. Add them up and you see that you are an instrument of ten strings to be used to praise God."

This is doubtless faulty exegesis of the psalm but it comes close to what Paul had in mind when he said, "Present your bodies as a living sacrifice, holy and acceptable to God" (Romans 12:1). And it is the secret of the liberal giving by the Macedonians who "first gave themselves to the Lord" (2 Cor. 8:5).

A Christian is God's instrument and his whole life is a psalm of thanksgiving to God.

T. A. Kantonen

66.   THE GREATEST MOMENT

A few years ago a reporter interviewed Marion Anderson and asked her to name the greatest moment in her life. She has many big moments to choose from. There was the night Toscanini told her that hers was the finest voice of the century. There was the private concert she gave at the White House for the Roosevelts and the King and Queen of England. To top it all, there was that Easter Sunday in Washington when she stood beneath the Lincoln statue and sang for a crowd of 75,000 which included Cabinet members, Supreme Court Justices and most members of Congress. She chose none of these. Miss Anderson told the reporter that the greatest moment in her life was the day she went home and told her mother she wouldn't have to take in washing any more!

L. E. Smith

67.   A GLASS OF BUTTERMILK

An illustration furnished by Mr. Robert Jolly, administrator of the Memorial Hospital located at Houston, Texas, beautifully reveals the returns which Christian hospitals are giving back in service for what they are costing:

A noted surgeon from Baltimore had his summer home in the mountains of Virginia. It was his custom while occupying this home to tramp daily through the mountains. On a hot day in August he came upon a little cabin in a cove, and, being tired from his walk, and thirsty, he asked a little girl at a mountain cabin if she would give him a drink of water. She asked him if he would not like to have some milk, stating that they had milk in the springhouse. The great surgeon assured her that he had rather have some buttermilk just then than anything he could think of. So the little girl gave him a large goblet of milk.

Winter came and the surgeon went back to his practice in Baltimore. Later the little girl was stricken with appendicitis. The mountain doctor advised that she go to Baltimore for an operation. The father sold their cow to get sufficient money to go to the city. When the surgeon came to operate on the child, lo and behold, he was the man to whom she had given the buttermilk.

After a few days the child began to recover and then to worry how they were to pay the hospital and surgeon's bill. When her father came each day to see her she would begin to fret about how they would pay. The father tried in every way he knew to cause her not to worry, but knowing their circumstances as she did, the hospital bill was ever on her mind. Finally the day came when she was to be discharged. Her father came as usual to see her, and the first thing she asked was, "Have you gotten the bill?" Then she said, "Father, maybe I could get a job in Baltimore when I get well and pay these folks for all they have done for me."

While they were talking, a representative of the hospital came in and handed the father a statement of all the expense. Anxiously the little girl glanced at it with him and saw these items:

14 days at $3.50 per day	$49.00
Laboratory	5.00
Drugs and dressings	5.00
Total	$59.00

Right under the total was written:

Surgeon's fee $250.00

Then the child broke into tears and wailed, "Why, daddy, we could never get that much money together. What in the world shall we do?"

And the father replied, "But, Gladys, look down at the bottom. You didn't read it all!" And down at the bottom were these words: Paid for with a glass of buttermilk. Signed, Howard A. Kelly.

H. W. Ellis

68.   GOD IN THE SOAP BUSINESS

Many years ago a lad of sixteen years left home to seek his fortune. All his worldly possessions were tied up in a bundle, which he carried in his hand. As he trudged along he met an old neighbor, the captain of a canal-boat, and the following conversation took place, which changed the whole current of the boy's life:

"Well, William, where are you going?"

"I don't know," he answered; "father is too poor to keep me at home any longer and says I must now make a living for myself."

"There's no trouble about that," said the captain. "Be sure you start right, and you'll get along finely."

William told his friend that the only trade he knew anything about was soap and candle making, at which he had helped his father while at home.

"Well," said the old man, "let me pray with you once more, and give you a little advice, and then I will let you go."

They both kneeled down upon the tow-path (the path along which the horses which drew the canal-boat walked); the dear old man prayed earnestly for William, and then gave this advice: "Some one will soon be the leading soap-maker in New York. It can be you as well as any one. I hope it may. Be a good man; give your heart to Christ; pay the Lord all that belongs to him of every dollar you earn; make an honest soap;

give a full pound, and I am certain you will yet be a prosperous and rich man."

When the boy arrived in the city, he found it hard to get work. Lonesome and far from home, he remembered his mother's words and the last words of the canal-boat captain. He was then led to "seek first the kingdom of God and his righteousness," and united with the church. He remembered his promise to the old captain, and the first dollar he earned brought up the question of the Lord's part. In the Bible he found that the Jews were commanded to give one-tenth; so he said, "If the Lord will take one-tenth, I will give that." And so he did; and ten cents of every dollar were sacred to the Lord.

Having regular employment, he soon became a partner; and after a few years his partners died, and William became the sole owner of the business.

He now resolved to keep his promise to the old captain; he made an honest soap, gave a full pound, and instructed his bookkeeper to open an account with the Lord, and carry one-tenth of all his income to that account. He prospered; his business grew; his family was blessed; his soap sold, and he grew rich faster than he had ever hoped. He then gave two-tenths, and prospered more than ever; then he gave three-tenths, then four-tenths, then five-tenths.

He educated his family, settled all his plans for life, and gave all his income to the Lord's work. He prospered more than ever.

This is the story of Mr. William Colgate, who has given millions of dollars to the Lord's cause, and left a name that will never die.

Basil Miller

69.   OFF DEAD CENTER

An example which reveals both the imperative need and the glorious results which would follow worthy and cooperative effort among our churches comes to me in the memory of earlier years. When he was just a boy in his early teens, the writer worked for a time in a large factory where several hundred workmen were employed in making barrel heads. Sometimes in getting ready to start the day's work, the great engine that drove the machinery for all the mill would "stick on center": the steam pressure became equalized in the cylinders of the engine, and the great iron arm that turned the main shaft of the mill remained helpless and motionless. In such an hour there was but one thing to do: the engine must be rolled off center. Engineer Wade sent out a call to the workmen gathering for the day's work to "turn her over." From all parts of the building men gathered in the engine room. Every man was in his place: some seized the great iron fly wheel directly connected by a heavy belt to the main drive shaft; others took hold of the small belts that connected the drive shaft with individual machines. Every hand and heart was ready for the single task of throwing the helpless engine off center.

There was a moment of expectancy as all hands made themselves ready for a concerted effort; then came the lusty call of the engineer, "Turn her over!" Every back bent and every muscle bulged with strength that was given to a common task. Slowly the great drive wheel rolled over, and the mighty arm of the engine moved forward inch by inch; then, as the positions of the drive pistons were changed, came the hiss of inrushing steam supplied from the quadruple boilers. The task was done, and the engineer stood with his hand on the controlling throttle lest the power which had been helplessly imprisoned by its own neutralized strength hurl the monstrous engine into mad and calamitous runaway. Over and over turned the great machine in ever-increasing and rhythmic motion, till in every part of the factory, wheels buzzed, saw and planer knives bit into the seasoned wood, and the atmosphere was filled with happy activity.

There was no lack of power as the engine lay helpless and motionless. Men and machines were idle for a single reason:

the problem was not movingly linked with power. Until the shackles which held the engine in its grip were broken and the power which had been imprisoned in the boilers made free and sent on its mission of usefulness, all was in utter and hurtful stagnation.

H. W. Ellis

70.   WHY JAN DID NOT GRADUATE

On the day before school was to open four years ago, three white young people from Koinonia, Lora Browne, Jan Jordan and Bill Wittkamper, were notified that they would not be admitted to the white Americus High School. The School Board gave no explanation as to why these three were the only students from the county to be turned away. All efforts to get the Board to change its action failed. Finally, with the help of the American Civil Liberties Union, Koinonia won a Federal suit against the Board restraining it from barring these students because of the "religious and social beliefs" of their parents. They were ordered admitted, but no court has the power to change the climate of hostility with which they were surrounded.

This June all three graduated from high schools in different parts of the country. Bill Wittkamper, who transferred after one year in Americus, graduated from Evanston, Ill. Lora Browne, whose family (Con and Ora Browne) moved to Knoxville, Tenn., just before her senior year, was graduated from a high school there. Jan Jordan put in all four years at Americus High and intended to graduate very quietly. It didn't happen that way.

Like other seniors, she invited her friends to the graduation.

Unlike other seniors, some of her friends were Negroes. When they arrived at the gate of the stadium, where the exercises were to be held, they were turned away by police and school authorities. Once again all negotiations failed, and Jan, who was then in her cap and gown waiting for the procession to begin, was informed that her friends were not being admitted. She then stepped out of line, walked to the head of it and said to the faculty member in charge: "I think my friends have as much right to come to my graduation as anyone else's friends do." With this, she started walking toward the stands, where several thousand people were expectantly waiting for the procession to begin. They watched in amazement as this lone senior, followed by her father and kid brother (her mother stayed at the gate with those who had been barred), walked steadily toward them, slowly climbed to the top of the stands and sat down. Then the other seniors marched out on the field and seated themselves on the platform facing the stands—and Jan. After speeches by honor students on "Moral Responsibility" and "Reverence," each graduate was called to the rostrum and given a diploma. Jan's name was not called.

Next day, because she felt that some might not have understood her strange action the night before, Jan placed an ad in the Americus paper. It was headed: "WHY I DID NOT GRADUATE WITH MY CLASS AT AMERICUS HIGH," and stated simply that because her friends were not admitted on the same basis as other's, she felt unable to participate.

Following this, Koinonia challenged the right of the School Board to choose the friends of graduating seniors, and at the same time began pressing for immediate integration of the schools. Without going into all of the details, we might say simply that when the schools opened this fall, the Board had agreed to accept any Negro who applied, with no restrictions. There are now four Negroes enrolled in the Americus High School.

C. L. Jordan

71.   MY DUTIES TO MYSELF

David Livingstone spent many years of his life in Africa as
a missionary for Christ. When he was buried in Westminster
Abbey, thousands of people lined the streets of London to pay
respect to the memory of this great man of God. Among those
who were gathered to show their honor was a shabbily dressed
old man who wept bitterly. When someone inquired as to the
cause for his tears, he replied: "David and I were born in the
same village, brought up in the same school and Sunday school,
and worked together at the same loom. But David went that
way, and I went this; now he is honored by the nation, and I
am neglected, unknown and dishonored. I have nothing to look
forward to but a drunkard's grave."

                                              R. C. Rein

72.   ON BEING AN AMERICAN IN INDIA

Train travel in India is made difficult because of the increase
in passenger traffic due to industrialization, population growth
and the greater mobility which modernization brings. We
always carry with us our own bedding-roll. On the whole,
accommodations have been good. One night, however, when I
was traveling alone and had to change trains, I could get no
sleeping accommodation. Thinking I might have to sit up all
night, I started to step aboard the train and saw seven soldiers
blocking the passage. I ventured, "If there is floor space for a
bedding-roll, would one American crowd you too much?"
Immediately I was helped in. Two men began to roll up their
bedding to give me a choice of their bunks. Only over strong
protests did I maintain that my place was on the floor. On
another trip I shared a compartment with an army officer. "Are
you an American?" the officer asked me during the intro-

ductions. Then he added, "I am always glad to be with an American. We were very sad when we heard that your President was assassinated. We soldiers wept. Immediately we placed mourning bands on our arms and kept them on for twelve days. We do not forget how your country has helped us."

Paul R. Lindholm

TALENTS

73.   SHADE FOR A SUN-DIAL

Phillips Brooks once told a story of some savages to whom a sun-dial had been given. So desirous were they to honor it and keep it sacred that they housed it in and built a roof over it. We should be careful not to smile for great numbers of civilized people take many of God's gifts and treat them in just the way these untutored savages did the sun-dial. How many there are (who are not savages, save in this particular) who take God's gifts not to use for larger life but to keep and protect. So they put them in banks and in safety-deposit boxes. They house them in and build a roof over them. Those savages never did own that sun-dial. It was not something to use and profit by and serve with, but something to be kept, to be guarded, to be concerned about. They had, in a measure, to live for it not by it. So too often our gifts from God never belong to us. We have to keep them, care for them, worry about them. Nothing really belongs to us until we pass it on to some one else.

Guy L. Morrill

74. ON A DESERT ROAD

It is amazing how many times God is able to work a miracle on a desert road. There is something very suggestive in the fact that in this story of Philip's encounter with the Ethiopian eunuch, it is reported that it occurred on an out-of-the-way spot along a desert highway.

It was in a tiny little meeting, in a private home, among a small company of strangers, that John Wesley experienced his "heart-warming experience"—a spiritual miracle which set fires burning throughout the English-speaking world. It was in the quiet of his cell, alone with his New Testament, that Martin Luther elaborated the great light and truth that started the Protestant Reformation.

Read the biographies of the saints and the martyrs and it will begin to appear almost from the first page that God seems to have a marked preference for desert roads. It was at a lonely spot on the road to Damascus, you will remember, that St. Paul has his transforming experience.

This can hold true even in a city. In Chicago there is a Lutheran church which has had perhaps the most amazing success of any congregation in the city. Its church building is relatively small and its equipment is meager, but one service follows another through the entire sabbath day. Its activities crowd the calendar of every week. It has been necessary on occasion to rent the Civic Opera to house the congregation in excess of six thousand people. Throughout the year there is a veritable stream of money flowing from the church to needy spots across the world.

When pressed for an explanation of his remarkable success, the pastor said: "All I do is visit in the homes, meet the people face to face, persuade them to set up family altars, tithe, and dedicate their all. Then I go back within a few weeks to find out how they are getting along. I ask the treasurer for a report to see how they are coming with their giving. And I talk to the young people about becoming ministers and missionaries. It is all personal work."

On the desert highways of a great American city this man has worked a miracle, because God has gone down those same highways with him, preparing the way.

Roy L. Smith

75.   UPPER ROOM: FURNISHED

In the midst of a prayer meeting service in a large downtown church, with several hundred people present, a timid little woman arose to speak. It was in the midst of the Lenten season and the pastor had asked a rather simple but searching question: "Suppose you had the chance to be some one person associated with those last days of Jesus in Jerusalem, whom would you choose to be?" The woman was trying to reply to that question.

"There are a lot of people in the passion story whose place I could never fill," she said. "I could not carry my Master's cross as Simon of Cyrene did. Nor could I have followed him out to the garden as some of the others did. But I could make ready for him the best room in my house, where he might eat the last supper with his disciples. I could promise him that it would be made ready to his satisfaction." There was something very simple in her testimony, but those who knew the little woman were well aware of the truth in her words: ". . . it would be made ready to his satisfaction." She was that kind of person.

Someone had to make ready a room and furnish it. There is no record of any such thing in the scripture, but it is easy to imagine some housewife telling her Christian friends, years afterward, how the Lord had come to their home that night and had eaten that last solemn meal under her roof. She never wrote a gospel nor became a martyr, nor did she hold an office in the church; but she could provide a furnished room!

A great deal of the service of the kingdom of God (and the Church) must be rendered by those who never get their names into the papers, are never publicly commended, and are never elected as a delegate. But there is need for a furnished upper room and some devoted heart furnishes it without thought of publicity or commendation. In the eternal records of God the name is inscribed, and after it the notation—clearly written: "Well done, thou good and faithful steward."

Roy L. Smith

76.   SECOND FIDDLES ARE NEEDED TOO

The conductor of a great symphony orchestra on tour was being interviewed by a little girl reporter from the high school paper. She was a charming lass, with a great ambition to succeed, and no experience whatever with great artists.

"My editor would like to know," she began, with an evident effort to appear professional, "what instrument in the orchestra is the hardest to play."

Without a second's hesitation the great musician replied, "A second fiddle! And it's that way with life, too. It is always easy to find those who want to play the solos. It is something else to find those who are willing to provide the harmony and the accompaniment."

Roy L. Smith

77.   A WOMAN WITH AN IDEA

To Mary Lyon who pioneered in higher education for women the task of earning money proved one that took all her strength and courage; the wisdom to use it rightly took wisdom beyond her own thinking; the task to which she felt God had called her demanded the complete consecration of her physical resources, her mental powers, her spiritual strength, and her money—as well as that of any person she could interest in her "cause."

Mary Lyon. A strong name among the Christian women of America. She dreamed of a college for girls equal in all respects to the numerous colleges for men at a time when the very idea was almost a sacrilege. Then she made the dream come true.

Fifty years after the founding of Mount Holyoke Seminary (later changed to College) a trustee of the school expressed the almost universal attitude of the time: "It was an innovation uncalled for, unheard of until now since the foundation of the world . . . It was unnatural, unphilosophical, unscriptural, unpractical and impractical, unfeminine and anti-Christian . . . Had not Paul said, 'I suffer not a woman to teach nor to usurp authority over the man, but to be in silence; and if they will learn anything let them ask their husbands at home'? It would be the entering wedge to woman's preaching, practicing, lecturing, voting, ruling, buying and selling, doing everything that men do and perhaps doing it better than men do, and so overstocking all the trades and professions . . . At the same time it was insisted that such occupations as mathematics and philosophy were not suited to the tastes or capacities of women; they didn't want them and wouldn't undertake them; and if they did, they would ruin their health, impair their gentleness, delicacy, modesty, and refinement, unsex them and unfit them for their proper sphere." In the face of such prejudice Mary Lyon succeeded in doing the hitherto unattempted.

When, in 1834, her battle for a girls' college had progressed far enough that a few men of distinction and a few ministers agreed to meet with her to talk over possibilities, she realized that the campaign was hardly begun.

A thousand dollars was needed for a campaign fund. With clear logic she argued that if men were willing to support the many men's colleges and seminaries why should women not be eager to support a college for women? It seemed at first more logical than convincing. Few women had independent incomes in those days and the few who did were not generally devoted to doing good works, Miss Lyon discovered. So the money came from her co-workers in the Academy, from her former pupils, from her own purse, from mothers whom she could interest in the future of their daughters, and from working women who felt the spell of Miss Lyon's devotion to a great ideal. In less than two months she had raised almost the entire amount, at the same time carrying her full teaching load. The infant idea of a college for women took its first real breath and decided to live.

Difficulties dogged her footsteps. Finally, November 8, 1837, arrived and with it came the first college for women in America.

But in the minds of her pupils Miss Lyon was not primarily an organizer, an administrator, a money raiser, or a tradition breaker. She was a beloved friend. Under her influence the girls of Mount Holyoke were outstandingly Christian girls. Her pupils scattered as missionaries to all parts of the world. They cherished her words and her counsel. At one time she said, "How much happier you would be to live in a thousand lives beside yourself rather than to live in yourself alone! This throwing out of the whole soul in powerful, vigorous, disinterested action for others, no matter how self-denying, will make you receive a hundredfold in return. First, you must give yourself to Christ, and then go about like Him. He was never striving for a place where to live."

Among her notes are the outlines for many talks and in these the emphasis on giving bulks large. "We are not our own in the use of temporal things . . . We are to live for eternity in the use of money. This is possible. Many think it is not. Fix your eye on eternity just as it is. Every dollar you spend, cast your eye into eternity."

"To give in Christ's name, we must give as much as He requires. He will allow of no compromise. Ananias and Sapphira."

"We must have just views on Christ's poverty. No merit to be poor—none to be rich. But to be poor as Christ was is accepted."

"If we give in sacred charity, and give for Christ's sake, we must give so as to feel the loss of what we give continually. I dare not tell anyone how much to give; but I have no doubt of certain great principles of which this is one, that we ought voluntarily to submit to suffer in person and in feeling for Christ."

Harriet Harmon Dexter

78.   WORK THERAPY

A study was made of 402 persons aged ninety-five years and older. An effort was made to discover the cause of their longevity and to note any characteristics common to all of them. This one common trait was found: The ability to go about one's daily work without tension, worry, and anxiety. Work—within the limits of one's physical stamina—is never harmful. It is only the worry and tension that wears one down. One of the oldsters studied was 106 years of age. He had had a leg amputated when he was 102. Three prosthetic suppliers refused to fit him with an artificial limb, saying it would be a waste of money. In describing how he recovered, the oldster said, "They told me to get a wheelchair, and I told them to go to hell. I learned to walk the first time a hundred years ago and I could learn again." And he did!

Robert J. Hastings

79.   PROBLEM PEOPLE

The Christian Church is never more effective than when it is
a problem to secularism.

Martin Luther was a serious problem to the Roman Catholic
Church. His denunciation of the sale of indulgences, his recognized scholarship, his long years of devotion to the Church, and
his unassailable life of piety left his accusers helpless.

John Wesley was a problem to the ecclesiastics of his day.
His profound devotion to the cause of the poor, his strict devotion to the basic beliefs of the Protestant faith, and his utter
unselfishness, laid the burden of proof on his critics.

William Booth was a problem to his superiors. His desperate
concern for the lost, his flaming evangelistic passion, and his
complete indifference to his personal fortunes, made him invul-
nerable.

Of all the Protestant groups, none have been more of a problem to their Christian neighbors than the Quakers. Armed only
with good will and going out into every spot where there is
suffering and need, they have asked nothing for themselves. Yet
in all the annals of Christendom, no body of believers has suf-
fered more than have those who are content merely to be called
Friends.

Peter and John had the whole temple system completely
upset, for no better reason than that they had done a good
work in the name of a good man. When called to account, they
laid no claim to any honor for themselves, being quite content
to ascribe all honor to their lord. They did not even ask that
their pictures be published in the papers.

There is something rather bewildering about the man who
puts his all at the disposal of his Lord. He seems to work so
many miracles that cannot be explained. Albert Schweitzer, for
example! And Sir Wilfred Grenfell, up in Labrador! And
Kagawa, in the Kobe slums! Even Mahatma Gandhi had the
world wondering. John Calvin, John Knox, Savanarola, Eliza-
beth Fry, Roger Williams—how much did they leave? Who

can estimate the treasure they left behind them? Yet they were always a problem. For whatever it is worth, let us make note of the fact that none of these can be counted among the world's wealthy, though they are among the richest the world has ever known.

Roy L. Smith

80.   "STEWARD" IN DEAD SEA SCROLLS

At Qumran the three priests were assisted by overseers or *mebaqqerim* as well as the twelve laymen who formed part of the community council. These "overseers" would appear to correspond to the "presbyters" of Apostolic times, and among the sectaries the office was, with that of the presiding priest, one of the highest which the members of the religious community could hope to attain. The "overseer" presided over the sessions of "the Many," and exercised the offices of treasurer, director of sacred and secular labour, and supervisor of candidates for admission to the brotherhood. He was required to be devoted to the welfare of his charges "as a father loves his children," shepherding them in time of trouble. The concept of the shepherd as descriptive of leaders and overseers was an established Old Testament theme, and thus it is not surprising to read that Jesus spoke of Himself as "the good shepherd" and that one of His disciples applied the concept of the Christian Shepherd to Him.

Roland Kenneth Harrison

81.   ERASTUS: STEWARD

Northwest of Corinth, in the vicinity of two ruined theatres, a paving-block bearing an inscription in Greek was uncovered by American archaeologists. It stated that the pavement was the work of Erastus, who was at that time the *aedilis* or Commissioner of Public Works. This official is generally identified with the Erastus who became associated with Paul in the spread of the Gospel, and who was referred to in Romans as the *oikonomos* or "chamberlain" of the city.

Roland Kenneth Harrison

82. HEADED FOR JAIL

About thirty years ago a class in sociology at Johns Hopkins University made a careful, scientific study of one of the worst slum districts of Baltimore. The students went into the homes, noted all the good and bad influences in the community, and tabulated the results on cards. Two hundred cards were marked HEADED FOR JAIL. On each of these two hundred cards was the name of a boy or girl whose background, home surroundings, attitude toward life, and prospects indicated a life of crime, ending in jail or worse.

After a lapse of twenty-five years, another class in sociology in Johns Hopkins, searching for a project, found this bundle of cards marked HEADED FOR JAIL. The task of checking on every card was chosen by this class as their project for the year.

That class was headed for a surprise, for only two persons on the cards marked HEADED FOR JAIL ever got there. There was a reason that only two of those two hundred ever got to jail. The reason was Aunt Hannah. She was a schoolteacher in that particular slum section and taught in the grade school. The stories of the two hundred headed for jail ran true to the same pattern. One man, whom the second crew of investigators interviewed, said, "I sure was a bad egg. I was the worst kid in the neighborhood, and how the cops did like to pin anything and everything on me! They were usually right. One day Aunt Hannah kept me after school. She told me I was too smart a kid to be getting into trouble, and before I left she asked me to come to her home for dinner the next Sunday. I just never had the heart to let Aunt Hannah down after that; and now I'm a doctor in the same community."

Aunt Hannah, herself, could tell a great story, but this was all she would say to the investigators: "Oh, I just loved them like they were my own boys and girls. I just invested my time and talents and love in two hundred children, who by scientific prophecies, were headed for jail, and now look at them; all but two, the best citizens in Baltimore; church members, Protestants, Roman Catholics, and Jews. All good, substantial people."

Edwin A. Briggs

TITHING

83.   A TITHING TESTIMONY

In all these thirty years I have never seen the day when I was tempted for a moment to return to the old, spasmodic, haphazard method of giving to the Lord. We, too, have been blessed temporally and spiritually, in basket and in store, in mind and in heart, in this practice of systematic giving. There has seemed to be an overarching Providence all the way.

Charles R. Brown

84.   WHAT TITHING DOES

After starting to tithe, many have found that they have more funds on hand to devote to the work of God. They then experience in giving the joy Jesus promised in His words: "It is more blessed to give than to receive."

The superior discipline of systematically putting God first will contribute to quality of character to an extent that should make every parent who intelligently loves his children want them to be sincere tithers.

Tithing is a venture of faith and trust which leads to greater faith and trust, and this is a closer fellowship with God that drives away fear, and puts in its place lasting peace, strength and joy.

Tithing helps a man have more reverence for God, the "God of gods, and Lord of lords," preventing his from being sacrilegious to his worship.

Paul R. Lindholm

85.   "POOR JESUS"

A woman in a church in Arizona told me that she tried to teach her daughter the meaning of proportionate giving. She took ten pennies from her daughter's bank and laid them in a row. The mother said, "These are your ten pennies." She then put one penny aside and said, "This is for Jesus."

The young girl looked at the nine pennies, then at the one. She looked up at her mother, and glancing at the one lonely penny, said, "Poor Jesus!"

Curtis R. Schumacher

86.   ·   PROPORTION, NOT QUANTITY

Chinautla is a Pocoman Indian village not far from Guatemala City. One of the early converts, Dona Candelaria Sazo de Velasquez, after vainly seeking a cure for her disease among witch doctors, came to a group of evangelical Christians as a last resource. She was led by these friends to accept Christ as her Savior and soon found healing for both body and spirit. Since then she has been a devoted follower of Christ and a sacrificial giver. The mother of nine children, she helps her husband to support the family by making clay water jugs by hand. She can make one or two a day along with her other work, so at the end of the week she has about a dozen which she can sell for fifteen or twenty cents apiece. Out of her poverty she makes an offering to the Lord of fifty cents or more each week. She also gives one egg out of every ten, one chick out of every ten hatched, and the best fruits and flowers from her garden to help support her pastor. This Indian woman has discovered the secret of the blessing and the joy of sacrificial giving.

Guatemala News

87. KEEPING FAITH

A young clergyman and his wife, having agreed that they would tithe their family income, had paid their tenth regularly and meticulously throughout a period of two or three years.

There came a day when hospital bills, an expensive cross-country move, and one or two other emergency situations produced a financial crisis. For the first time in their young-married life they found themselves hard pressed for funds and faced a stern decision: Should they take the tithe out of their small salary as usual, or should they spend their pittance for their own needs and make an entry on their books that they "owed the Lord" the proportionate amount?

It was then that the young wife's faith came to the rescue. "When we agreed to tithe," she said, "we did not stipulate that we would pay the tenth in good times and hold out in bad times. How can we expect God to see us through if he can't count on us in dark days?" With that, they paid up their pledge.

Years afterward, in telling of this experience, the young husband said, "Nothing gave us so much assurance of the companionship of God during those days as the sure knowledge that we had kept faith with Him when all about us was dark."

Roy L. Smith

VALUES

88.   Missions and Mortgages

I was once introduced to a banker. He said he wasn't much of an Episcopalian, but that's all he was of anything. Though we had just met, he moved in bluntly on me and said, "We lend a lot of money to churches which are putting up new buildings. I can't persuade these other officers to go along with me, but if I could, I'd never lend a dime to a church unless the members promised not to give a cent to missions until they paid off our mortgage."

Though I think of myself as normally a mild-mannered person, once in a great while I'm surprised to overhear myself sounding a bit blunt. It was so that day. I said to him, "I'm neither a gambler nor a banker, but right now I wish I were both, for I'd take you till it hurt. I would bet you that you'd lose on every loan you'd make that way. If you teach people to be selfish, they'll wind up being selfish with the teacher. If you teach a church not to pay their obligations to the world, you'll soon discover you have taught them not to pay their obligations to the bank. If you teach them to think of themselves first before others, you'll have taught them to think of themselves before they think of you."

Dow Kirkpatrick

89.   IS GOLD WHERE YOU FIND IT?

Years ago a prospector came upon an abandoned gold mine. With a lantern and a pick he began to search the mine for one last vein which others might have overlooked.

Years later a party of engineers explored that abandoned mine. In the deepest shaft they came upon a little pile of rock and beside it a rusted pick. Farther along the shaft lay a battered lantern, and still farther, a human skeleton, its bony hand clutching one nugget of gold. The prospector had found his treasure, but lost his way.

Beware of seeking too long and too hard for that which has no value at all if a man loses his Way.

Henry B. Luffberry

90.   NAME NOT FOR SALE

General Robert E. Lee was once offered $10,000 a year for the use of his name in connection with a state lottery, at a time when money was a pressing necessity with him. His reply to those who made the proposal was, "Gentlemen, my name is all I have left, and that is not for sale."

Basil Miller

91.   DON'T BE A MONKEY

During World War II, I served in the United States Navy. Fortunately or unfortunately, most of my service was in San Diego so that my firsthand experiences of the war were not noteworthy; however, my job was such that I was privileged to hear many of the firsthand experiences of the sailors.

One of their stories intrigued me and has stuck in my memory ever since. It was a simple story of how the natives trap monkeys on the particular island that the sailor found himself on during the war. He told me that the natives would take earthen jars, with long narrow necks, and secure them to the trees that were the habitat of the monkeys. Then they would fill these jars with grain.

At night the monkeys came down from the trees and reached into the jars to get the grain; but when they tried to take their hands out of the jars, they found it impossible because they had a fistful of grain. All the monkeys needed to do was to turn loose the grain, but this they refused to do. They lost their liberty rather than turn loose their little fistful of grain.

Like the trapped monkeys, many Christians would rather hold onto their possessions and miss the kingdom than turn them loose and enjoy the freedom and abundance of the Kingdom of God.

Eugene F. Jud

92.   A YARDSTICK OF DEVOTION

"Greater love hath no man than this: that he lay down his life for his friends."

Lou Marsh read those words of Jesus when he was a boy attending a Baptist Sunday School. He took them—as most Christians do—as a yardstick of ultimate devotion. He had no way of knowing, then, that he would one day be measured against that yardstick.

In hindsight, it seems rather a miracle that Lou Marsh should have had any love at all in him—let alone the supreme kind of love. He was a quiet, serious-minded Negro boy, more sensitive than most to the humiliations and deprivations which were visited upon him while he was growing up in one of Philadelphia's black ghettoes. Somehow he survived all of the hurts without learning to hate. By the time he had won admission to Temple University, he had made up his mind to devote his life to some kind of Christian service to mankind.

He was graduated from Temple and spent two years at Yale Divinity School, preparing for the ministry. Then, like many young seminarians, he began to have doubts about his vocation. He felt that he had been called to follow Christ, but he was not sure exactly how or where. So he decided to leave school for a while and work.

Last May, he got a job as a social worker with New York City's youth board. He was assigned to work with "the young untouchables," a gang of Negro and Puerto Rican teen-agers in one of the toughest slums of East Harlem. What happened after that is recorded in this week's *Christian Century* magazine by Dean Peerman, an associate editor who was a seminary classmate of Lou Marsh.

> Lou soon developed a strong attachment to the gang members, identifying with them and their troubles . . . and he had a large measure of success with his boys. He had won their confidence and respect, he was 'getting through' to them. It was a dangerous job, and when Marsh went home to Philadelphia for a brief Christmas vacation, his mother urged him to give it up and go back to Yale.
>
> I'll be all right, he assured her. I can take care of myself. Besides, somebody has to do the job.

Last month, word reached Marsh that the "young untouchables" were squaring off for a rumble with "the playboys," a rival gang which had invaded their territory. The crisis developed suddenly on the night of January 7. There was no time to call the police, so Marsh acted on his own to cool off the situation. He walked into a war council of the "young untouchables" and persuaded them to abandon the planned fight. Then he started down the dark street toward his room.

On the way he was ambushed by four older boys, "graduates" of the gang who resented his influence with the boys and his success in preventing the rumble. Two held his arms while the other two beat him senseless. A passerby found him lying in the street and called an ambulance. But he died in the hospital without ever regaining consciousness.

> Lou would not want to be called a martyr, says his friend, Dean Peerman. But there is no gainsaying that Lou died as a Christian doing his duty.

From a human perspective, it seems a terrible waste that a man like Lou Marsh should lay down his life, at the age of 29, on a dirty slum street in East Harlem. But the One from whom he took his cue died on a smelly Palestine hillside at the age of 33, and there have been few who have thought during the past 20 centuries that either his life or his death were a waste.

Louis Cassels

93.   FORTUNE AT A SACRIFICE

Three brothers owned a profitable business in a Tennessee city. They were making a comfortable living and were considered successful businessmen, though none of them was really wealthy. A concern which had a selling proposition, but neither the capital nor the equipment to finance it, offered to sell the brothers a controlling interest in the new enterprise if they would take it over. They considered the matter and agreed that they could easily make a million dollars on the new venture and could make it fairly and honestly. The next day, the man who had made the proposition was amazed when they turned it down.

When pressed for the reason, the men admitted that it

would pay. "But," said one of the brothers, "we are men of
families and officials in our church. With our present volume
of business we can provide for our families and do our part
toward religious, educational, and charitable enterprises. When
the day's work is over, we can forget our business and give our
evenings to our families, our church, or our community. If we
take over such an increased volume of business, it means longer
hours of work, which would leave no time for our children and
no time for our church. We have decided that these are values
which money cannot buy. We would be untrue to our stewardship if we made a fortune at the sacrifice of our service to our
church and of our family life."

Ina C. Brown

94.   We Are All Debtors

A friend described what he said was the most remarkable
experience of his life. It was the discovery of his own mother
when he was thirty years of age. Now, my friend had not been
an orphan nor had there been any separation from his mother
in the early years of his life. On the contrary, he had grown up
in a fine home under his mother's daily care. He had gone to
school and college; and, when he made the discovery of his
mother, he was happily married and well-established in a useful
profession. Then, one day, almost dramatically, there came to
him a sudden realization of who his mother really was. She
was still alive, but, somehow, he saw her for the first time in
his life as she really was in her true character. He saw her as a
gracious and loving woman, who, in the pain of birth, had
brought him into life, who had fed and bathed him as a helpless infant, who had taken such delight in his first toddling steps,
who had treasured his first spoken words as the sweetest music,
who had watched over him day by day with such tender care

and prayed for him every night; who had taken such pride in his success. All of this my friend had taken in a careless spirit of acceptance with hardly a thought. Then, in a flash of revelation, as a grown man, there came to him who his mother really was. It was a deeply moving experience. In fact, he maintained, it changed his entire outlook on life.

This was how my friend made the momentous discovery that we are all debtors. We are born in debt, and we continue to live in debt. Human existence is a debtor economy.

James S. Thomson

95.   SHORT MEASURE

The story is told of a miller who asked an apple grower, "How is it when I measured the five barrels of apples you sold me last week I was almost a barrel short?" "That's a fair question," the apple grower replied. "All I did was to send them to you in five of your own flour barrels."

George McNeill Ray

96.   "SYMPATHY ON THE CHEAP"

My first pastorate after graduation was a rural congregation in Ontario, Canada, in an area composed of descendants of Northern Ireland settlers who were hard-working, devout, and frugal.

One of the village physicians was Dr. Ferguson, a bluff-speaking, able and active man of over sixty years, who had a large practice covering a wide territory and responded to both day and night calls.

One bitterly cold and snowy night the doctor was called to a remote part of the county where a poor farmer's wife was in birth pains. Despite a long day's work he set out in his cutter in the darkness over the poor roads on his mission of mercy. The birth was a complicated one, and just before the break of day the mother, in giving a life to the world, died. The husband was distraught, and it was with a heavy heart that Dr. Ferguson drove back to the village.

Tired and sad, he hitched his team to a post and entered the main store where a group of men were gathered around the big stove. He stamped the snow from his feet, unbelted his fur coat, and told the story of the tragedy of the practically destitute farmer, newly widowed, and with a new-born babe to care for. Voices were raised in sympathy. "What a pity!" was repeated over and over by the members of the group. The doctor's eyes traveled around the faces of the vocal sympathizers. Suddenly he whipped off his old fur cap and said, "Boys! How much is your sympathy worth?"

It's easy for us to speak sympathetically of the veteran retired ministers who laboured over many years for small salaries, and of our missionaries who have so sacrificially given themselves to the work of the kingdom of God in remote areas of the world. The question that will not down is the one posed by the old doctor: "How much is your sympathy worth?

James W. Clarke

97.   VALUES TRANSFORMED

It was just after ten o'clock on the night of April 14, 1912, that the *Titanic*, the largest vessel then afloat, crashed in mid-Atlantic into an iceberg, and four hours later went to the bottom. Much has been written of all that took place in those four hours. Survivors spoke of the calm heroism of the captain, the officers, and the crew. They told also of the courage of the bandmaster who played "Nearer, My God, to Thee," while he struggled into his life belt, and they said that many women, who could have been rescued, refused the offer, preferring to drown with their husbands.

They told another story also, less courageous but more curious than any of these.

A certain woman, who had been allotted a place in one of the boats, asked if she might run back to her stateroom, and she was given three minutes to go. She hurried along the corridors already tilting at a dangerous angle, and crossed to the saloon. Money and costly gems littered the floor. Some who snatched at their jewelry spilt it as they ran. In her own stateroom she saw her treasures waiting to be picked up. She saw— and took no heed. Snatching at three oranges which she knew to be there, she took her place in the boat.

That little incident is instructive. An hour before, it would have seemed incredible to that woman that she could have preferred a crate of oranges to one small diamond, but Death boarded the *Titanic* and, with one blast of his awful breath, all values were transformed. Precious things became worthless; worthless things became precious. Oranges were more than diamonds.

W. E. Sangster

98.   HOLDING OUR MINDS TO THE HIGHEST

Since time is such an elastic thing, God can help us to make time by crowding more experience into certain magic moments. Oh, I do not mean by rushing around fussing with more things. We can compute man-hours of manual labor, but who can say how much thought and feeling can be put into an hour? We can open our hearts and minds to a greater flow of thought and emotion. Recall how Handel composed "The Messiah." For twenty-four days he was completely withdrawn from the things of this world. So immersed was he in his music that the food brought to him sometimes was left untouched. Describing his feeling when the Hallelujah Chorus burst from his mind, Handel said, "I did think I did see all Heaven before me and the great God himself." We ordinary mortals have not the sensitivity or capacity of a Handel, but we can have our high moments, when we feel that "one crowded hour of glorious life is worth an age without a name." If we hold our minds to the highest we know and open our hearts to the best we can feel, God fills our minutes with magic content.

Ralph W. Sockman

99.   No Television Set

In San Francisco there was a family of five—father, mother, and three children. For several years they had wanted a television set and one recent Christmas they held a family council. They decided not to exchange Christmas gifts. Instead, they voted to pool the money they would spend upon each other and with this buy a television set. This would be a Christmas gift for everyone.

The next morning the seven-year-old son said to his father, "Dad, I didn't sleep well. I was thinking about what we decided last night. If we buy the television, does that mean I can't get you something for Christmas?"

"That's right," the father said.

"I can't give mother something?"

"That's what we decided."

"I can't get something for Susan and Helen?"

"Not if we buy the television set."

"Dad," the boy said, "I don't want a television set."

Curtis R. Schumacher

100.   INSIGHT

Moreover, we can make time by living with the *values that grow richer*. Somewhere I have heard the saying, "Even a fool can count the apples on a tree, but it takes a wise man to count the trees in an apple." To see the tree in the seed and then help it to grow; to pick the winner before he has won his laurels and then help him to win; to discover the poet or genius in that dreamy, restless, nonconforming schoolboy, and then help him to find himself—that is the creative kind of wisdom which keeps life growing and entitles us to be called "workers together with God."

Ralph W. Sockman

101.   BUILDING FOR WHOM?

In Edwin Markham's *Parable of the Builders*, we have the story of a certain rich man who had it in his heart to do good. One day, as he was walking out over his broad estate, he came to a little house down in a hollow where lived a carpenter with a very large family. The rich man sent for the carpenter and put before him the plans of a beautiful house and said, "I want you to build a house just like this over on that sunny hill. I want you to build it good and strong. Employ only the best workmen, and use only the best materials, for I want it to be a good house." Then he went away on a long journey and left it all to the builder. And after the rich man had gone, the carpenter said to himself, "This is my chance." So he used poor materials and gave poor workmanship that he might make more money for himself. At length, the rich man returned, and the carpenter brought him the keys, and said, "That is a fine house I built for you over on the sunny hill." "Good," said the rich man, "I am glad it is a good house. I have intended all along to give it to you when it was finished. The house is yours." The builder was heartbroken. How industriously he had been cheating himself. He took the keys and walked away, and muttered to himself, "Oh, if only I had known that I was building the house for myself."

Ralph W. Sockman

102.　　　　RELEVANT LIVING

A bride of a few months listened to two members of her husband's family deciding who were the happiest couple they knew. The decision for first place went to a cousin and his wife. A little surprised at first, she studied the situation. She found that the happiest-couple-in-the-world had the lowest income of any of the brothers and sisters in the family. She found that they lived in the smallest house; they knew the fewest big-name people; their professional work drew the least national recognition. But she also discovered that they had jobs which were their choice of any in the world; they liked their community; they lived in the part of the United States they loved most; their home was the center of informal friendly groups; they had more interests on the string than a dozen people could conquer in a lifetime; they instigated many community and church activities. The young bride came to the decision that this couple was happy not because of the money they did not have, and not because of the money they did have, but because the interests around which their lives centered were interests that money had no power to make or break. Their greatest happiness was found outside the realm of things.

Harriet H. Dexter

103.   PROVE AND IMPROVE

I heard of a man who was offered a deal in which there was a chance to make a great deal of money. He looked it over, then at luncheon he explained to the company representative that he could not take it. When pressed for his reason, he said, "I am a Christian man, my company tries to do business by Christian principles, and in the light of that I can see no possible way to handle this." The other businessman looked at him in amazement and said, "Surely you don't try to mix two good things like business and religion." Then from across the table he heard an expression which should be inscribed over every business. "My friend, I have discovered that it is only when we do mix business and religion that we can prove our religion and improve our business."

J. Wallace Hamilton

104.   NIBBLING THEMSELVES AWAY

An old shepherd once said, "There is nothing vicious about a sheep. He does not go off storming into the desert, nor does he climb some mountainside out of sheer wickedness. Instead, he just nibbles himself away. He gets so much interested in the tuft of grass that is just ahead of his nose that he eats himself off the trail before he knows it."

The number of actually wicked people in the world is probably not large. They get into the headlines and attract a great deal of attention, but they are a very small minority of the total population. The vast majority of those who get into serious trouble—those who get lost—are people who "just nibble themselves"off the trail.

They become so interested in that little extra profit, that additional sale, a few more votes, an extra convenience or two for the home, one more record broken, that they lose their sense of proportion. They allow trifles to blind them to the magnificences of life.

A young theological student and his wife, who set out for the seminary without sufficient funds to pay their first year's expenses, became so engrossed in earning "a little extra" that they skimped their school work. The next year, in order to make up some work, they both took additional courses and worked even a little more on the outside. When the strain became acute they became irritable with one another, each confiding in a friend that he did not believe the other appreciated him. Before the end of the year their home was in serious jeopardy and serious damage had been done to their spiritual life. This was reflected in an unhappy experience in their first church and, eventually, a divorce. They had nibbled themselves away.

The prophet says that most of us—all of us, in fact—go astray at least to some extent by this method. Beginning with a minor compromise, we go on to greater indiscretions. Rebelling against God in little things, we begin defying him in the basic matter. The tufts of grass just ahead of our noses seem so seductive.

Roy L. Smith

105.   THE NEED TO BE NEEDED

During the night of a flash flood in Connecticut, Norman Cousins drove through the night and into the middle of the morning, hoping to get through to the place where his daughter had been trapped in the storm. As he drove along, the headlights of his car caught the figure of a man in a yellow raincoat standing in the pounding rain. He held aloft an electric lantern, waving the car to a stop, and reported that a small bridge just beyond the turn in the road had been washed out. He was not a policeman or official of any kind. Earlier in the evening, he had learned that the bridge hadn't held and had attempted to notify the police. Unable to do so, he had decided to spend the rest of the night as a human warning station.

As he drove on, Mr. Cousins found people from nearby homes, some of them without raincoats or boots, working to help those who were stranded. Long past midnight, improvised rescue squads were at work everywhere. Each home on the road became something of a rescue station.

Looking back over the experiences of the night, Mr. Cousins said there was one recollection that stood out above all others: it was of the people themselves. Their heroism had been real, but there was something more important and memorable than that: it was the way the people looked as they worked during the storm. Something was coming through you didn't see very often, and it had an electric quality to it. The man in the yellow raincoat and hundreds of others who worked through the night didn't have the look of people who were satisfying their craving for excitement or hunger. They looked as though they were fulfilling something far more essential—the need to be needed. They had been made necessary in the lives of other people and they were acting on it, and it had given them satisfaction and warmth.

If someone were to ask, why is the church concerned about stewardship, I think the answer, in part, is to be found in the need of people to be needed. Deep within every one of us is the need to feel that we are needed.

Source unknown.

106.   THE RESPONSIBLE MAN

Count Saint-Exupéry was a philosopher, writer, poet, adventurer, and famous flyer. His books are widely read, the most famous of which is "*Wind, Sand and Stars.*" In it he tells that after World War I, with his flying comrade Guillaumet, he went to South America where the two men secured jobs as pilots carrying the mails over the Andes for the government of Chile.

One day Guillaumet, despite a heavy snowstorm which had bottled up all space, had taken off in the hope of finding a rift in the sky. To his dismay he discovered he was trapped within a circle of peaks twenty thousand feet high, and that great downdrafts were beating him lower. His wings were icing heavily; the jolts of the turbulence were so terrible that his seat harness threatened to snap, and his plane was being rolled over and under like a hat in the road, from eighteen thousand feet down to ten. Spying a frozen lake at the bottom, he flew around it until his gas was exhausted, and finally was able to set the ship down on the snow.

Because of the fierceness of the storm he dug a shelter beneath his cockpit, lined it with mail bags, and huddled there for two days and nights. Then he emerged to find his way back to civilization, which took him five days and four nights, for he was without ice-ax, ropes, and food. He had to scale places fifteen thousand feet in the air and crawl on the face of almost vertical slopes, hands and feet bleeding, in a temperature of twenty degrees below zero.

Longing to lie down, the thought of his wife and sons, who would be left penniless if he perished, and his responsibility for the mail, kept him struggling forward with the pertinacity of an ant, despite the petrifying cold and the agony of his frozen face, hands, and feet. He was finally found, but on examination at the nearest hospital it was discovered his hands and feet were so solidly frozen that a double amputation was necessary. Thus he lost the beautiful tools of his livelihood.

Saint-Exupéry, brooding over his comrade's awful experience and the dynamic which kept him walking, staggering, and crawling ever forward, summed up his conclusion in a single sentence, "To be a man is, precisely, to be responsible."

This is a direct and inescapable challenge to every church member at this season when the stewardship of time, service, and money is presented. "To be a Christian is, precisely, to be responsible."

He that hath ears to hear, let him hear.

James W. Clarke

107.   NO TIME TO LOOK UP

It is possible to be so constantly on the jump that all sight of goals is lost, all sense of adequateness is wiped out, and all channels to the source of power are clogged. There is terrible danger in this age of great activity that we will forget that time taken out for meditation, for the appreciation of the beautiful, for communion with God, is actually time put in to the best advantage. In Southern Illinois a young woman went into an Italian community to serve as a community counselor during her summer vacation. She located an old store building to use for a Vacation School and while she was busily sweeping it out with the help of a little Italian girl she looked out the door right into a flaming sunset. "Tonia," she said, "did you ever see anything so beautiful?" The little girl stood transfixed for a moment then suddenly darted down the step calling back, "I must run tell my mother." "But your mother can see it herself," said the counselor. The little girl stopped just long enough to say, "Oh, no—my mother never thinks to look up."

Harriet Harmon Dexter

108.   SAVING SELF

Many years ago a twenty-five-year-old nephew of Dr. Gansaulus, famous Chicago preacher, admitted his distress because he could find no purpose for his life. His uncle talked with him of the need to give himself for others as a means whereby such purpose could be found.

As he left the office, the young man noted that the old Iroquois Theatre was burning. He saw several people trapped in an upper-story window. Quickly he found a plank, climbed to a level in the next building where he placed the plank across to the window and helped several to safety. Unfortunately, a falling beam struck him and knocked him to the pavement far below. Dr. Gansaulus was called and arrived just before his nephew died. The young man looked squarely into his uncle's eyes and whispered, "Now I know why I was born."

Several years later Dr. Gansaulus fell to talking with another traveler in a hotel in Europe. A casual remark about Chicago so excited this man that he babbled unintelligibly; whereupon his companion led him away, explaining later to the minister that the man had been in the old Iroquois Theatre in Chicago on the fateful day it burned. He had managed to get out only by crawling and clawing his way over many screaming, fear-crazed, panic-striken people. Ever since, at the slightest reference to Chicago, he would tremble and mutter, "I saved nobody but myself, I saved nobody but myself." What a graphic revelation of the truth, "Whoever would save his life will lose it!"

Leslie R. Smith

109.   GRACE ABOUNDING

At a meeting of a service club, the members were attempting to secure the interest of more of the members in their special project. So they decided to dramatize the support they were giving to boy's work. They set up two head tables. At one of them they seated those men who through the years had devoted themselves wholeheartedly to this work. At the other table were men who, as boys, had benefited from the efforts of the service club.

As the men at the second table were introduced, it became clear that each of them was now making a particular contribution to the community through his life. It was a most effective object lesson. To use the language of the Bible, one would say that the grace bestowed on those boys by the club members had borne fruit in the men whose lives, in turn, had become further channels of a similar grace to other people.

—Author unknown

110.   ROMAN PERSECUTIONS

Late in 249 or early in 250 Decius issued an edict which provided that every inhabitant of the empire, without exception, should offer sacrifice to the gods. Some freedom of choice was permitted. In one of the acts of the martyrs the non-sacrificing Christian is offered his choice among Apollo, Jupiter, and Juno, and in another he is asked to sacrifice to Diana. The gods involved are Roman gods, however.

Certificates of sacrifice were issued by local commissions, and a good many of these have been found in Egypt. One of the most interesting was issued to a priestess of the crocodile god of Egypt:

> To the commission chosen to superintend the sacrifices. From Aurelia Ammonous, daughter of Mystus, of the Moeris quarter, priestess of the god Petesouchos the Great, the Ever-Living, and priestess of the gods in the Moeris quarter.

I have sacrificed to the gods all my life and without interruption, and now again, in accordance with the decree and in your presence, I have made sacrifice and poured a libation and partaken of the sacred victims.
I request you to certify this below.

The edict of Decius met with general approval, but Christians were often content to buy a certificate without sacrificing. The result was a deep split within the Christian church. The bishops, most of whom had neither sacrificed nor bought certificates, were scandalized with the behavior of those who had. And since most of the bishops had discreetly withdrawn to safety in exile, their criticisms of certificate buyers were not readily accepted.

There were, however, a few martyrs, including Fabianus, bishop of Rome. At Pergamum the bishop Carpus was burned alive, with two staunch supporters, though not before April of 251, and in May of the same year a certain Maximus, who refused to sacrifice to Diana, was stoned to death at Ephesus. The same proconsul, Flavius Optimus, had to deal with both cases.

Robert M. Grant

111.   CHURCH OR MAUSOLEUM

On a high hill near the outskirts of a midwestern city stands a structure which resembles a church building. The stately edifice has stood on the promontory for many years but never once has there been any mention from a pulpit of need for money or for a program of stewardship education and commitment.

Only on exceptional occasions do people enter the building, for usually it is securely locked and entered only by the man who serves as keeper of the grounds. When the doors are opened to the public the caretaker sweeps out the building, carefully cleans and waxes the floors, and polishes the brass and gold ornaments, of which there are many.

These are always occasions of sadness. For you see, this chapel was built for the dead and not for the living. Years ago a very wealthy family erected the building which has the appearance of a church and equipped it with all the furnishings of a church; but it is used only as a family crypt. It is opened only for funerals when the dead are buried beneath the floor. Having the form of a church building but in reality being a mausoleum, there is no need for a program of stewardship education and commitment.

Julian E. Stuart

112.   OUR WORLD IN MINIATURE

If in imagination we compress the present population of the world, now over two and a half billion, into a group of a thousand persons living in a single town, the following is the picture of contrasts we would then vividly see.

Sixty persons would represent the U.S. population: all others would be represented by 940. The 60 Americans would have half the total income of the entire town; the 940 would share the other half.

Thirty-six of the Americans in the town would be Christian Church members and 24 would not. In the town as a whole, about 300 would be Christians and 700 would not. At least 80 persons in the whole town would be believing Communists and 370 would be under Communist domination. Possibly 70 in the whole town would be Protestant Christians.

Three hundred and three persons in the whole town would be white; 697 would be non-white. The 60 Americans would have an average life expectancy of 70 years; all the other 940 would average under 40.

The Americans would have 15½ times as much per person as all the rest on an average. They would produce 16 percent of the town's total food supply, eat up 14½ percent of that total supply and keep most of the remaining 1½ percent for their future use in expensive storage equipment. When it is remembered that most of the 940 non-Americans in the town would always be hungry and never know quite when they would get enough to eat, the situation created by this disparity in food supply and the existence of vast reserves becomes fairly apparent, particularly in view of the fact that the Americans already eat 72 percent above the optimum food requirements. They could actually save money by giving away excess food because of the cost of storing it; but they think that would be a dangerous "give-away program of soft-headed do-gooders."

The 60 Americans would have, of the town's total supply: 12 times as much electric power as all the rest; 22 times as much coal; 21 times as much petroleum; 50 times as much steel and 50 times as much in general equipment.

The lowest income groups among the 60 Americans would be better off than the average in much of the rest of the town.

Literally most of the non-American people in the town would be poor, hungry, sick, and ignorant. Almost half would not be able to read or write.

More than half would never have heard of Christ or what he stood for. But very soon more than half would be hearing about Karl Marx.

In view of these facts it is interesting to think that the average Christian American *family* would be spending $850 a year for defense in force, and less than $3.50 a year to share with the rest of the people in the town the knowledge of why there is any Christmas.

Henry Smith Leiper

WILLS

113. OTHER PEOPLE'S CHILDREN

Leland Stanford lost his only child. Though he was United States Senator from California, he said to himself, "I have nothing to live for. I have no children." He put a million dollars into a private home, but it was not a home to him. One night he had a dream. In this dream his son appeared to him and said: "Father, never say again that you have nothing to live for—live for humanity, live for other people's children." There soon arose at Palo Alto the Leland Stanford Junior University at a cost of $20,000,000. He and Mrs. Stanford became the devoted servants of the poor, the orphan, and the suffering, and left all their property to go on doing good to the rising generations.

Julius Earl Crawford

114. THE WILL: NOBLEST OF RECORDS

I esteeme wills . . . to be of the noblest sort of recordes; for yt they acquaint us with more circumstances (and at the

least with no lesse certainty) then other recordes comonly do.
As namely, the substance of the deceased especially in his per-
sonall estate, his wife, children, kindred, servants and his
esteemed freindes (for of such consists his executors, super-
visers, and legatees) his inclinations to piety, charity and bounty,
the circumstantiall time (for the most part) of his death and
the place of buriall; all wch give much light and satisfaction to
such as listen after the memory of their ancestors.

Gervase Holles
(15th Century)

115.　　He Made His Money Immortal

In 1856, a successful merchant by the name of Maxwell
Chambers, who lived in Salisbury, North Carolina, gave the
sum of approximately one quarter of a million dollars to his
local church and to Davidson College, which was located about
twenty miles away. At that time, his business was one of
dominant influences and institutions in the entire community.
One can go back to Salisbury today and look in vain for the
slightest trace of his business or his life, except for what he
decreed in his will for Christian uses. There is not a reference
to be found. All that is left in the entire community, bearing
upon the life of Maxwell Chambers, grows out of his devoted
stewardship to his Lord and Master. His church still profits by
his bequests. The large central Administration Building of
Davidson College, for over a hundred years has been named the
Chambers Building. Here is a man who made money immortal.

John R. Cunningham

116.   DEAD HANDS

The Christian steward in making his will should not try to
keep his dead hand, in perpetuity, on his bequests. Someone
recently cited a number of trust funds in which hundreds of
millions of dollars are tied up—unused and unusable—because
their original objectives are no longer attainable or are grotesque
or fantastic. "A certain Captain Randall went to Alexander
Hamilton in 1801 to have him draw up a will. Hamilton advised
him to leave his modest fortune to endow a home for aged
sailors. The Captain's modest estate consisted of $7,000 and a
good farm, containing an excellent orchard and market garden.
As the captain had been intelligent enough to pick a location
on Fifth Avenue, the trust fund now amounts to about $25,-
000,000. The annual income is $1,000,000 and the trustees
spend much of it trying to locate aged sailors, of the type
described in the will."

"Back in the days of the California gold rush, a worthy
mayor of St. Louis left his money in trust to aid distressed
travelers whose wagons broke down or whose bacon gave out.
Today this fund amounts to $1,000,000 and for more than fifty
years the trustees have not been able to find a single stranded
prairie schooner."

                                        Guy L. Morrill

117.   FLEXIBILITY

The good steward will avoid too constraining and too endur-
ing a control of funds left for trust purposes. Much may be
assigned to the intelligence and wisdom of properly chosen
Boards of Trustees. And it is becoming more and more a
moot question whether public weal does not require that trust
funds have limited existence. It is being advocated that such

funds should slowly be dissipated over a course of years; a certain percentage of the capital fund along with the interest being used each year during the designated age of the fund. The Christian steward should give without undue restriction letting the wisdom of succeeding generations direct its best use. Thomas Jefferson once observed, speaking of legacies left with ironclad provisions for their use: "There are those who suppose that preceding generations had the right to impose laws upon us unalterable by ourselves and that we, in like manner, can make laws and impose burdens on future generations which they have no right to alter; in fine, that the earth belongs to the dead and not to the living."

Guy L. Morrill

SENTENCE SERMONS

Lyle L. Baughman
John E. Herrmann
Roy L. Smith
Stanley I. Stuber
General Sources

STEWARDSHIP EXTRACTS

John E. Herrmann

(*Flavors*: Vanilla, Lemon, Peppermint and Butterscotch)

I. GENERAL STEWARDSHIP

You can't live the new life with the old heart.

The man who thought up the eraser sure knew the human race.

98

Martin Luther once said: "If anyone raps at my heart and asks: 'Who lives here?', I reply: 'Martin Luther once lived here, but he has moved out, and Jesus Christ has moved in.'"

Giving God less than my whole life is robbery.

Life's greatest transaction: Jesus gave himself for me; I give myself to Him.

God must work in us if he is to work through us.

Many a self-made man just quit too early.

A conservative is one who does not think anything should be done the first time.

Air castles are nice until you step out.

Two critical changes in a man's life: 1) When his voice changes; 2) When his choice changes.

II. GIVING

How a Church raises money is more important than how much it raises.

What Christ calls for we cannot afford to keep.

Men live in their gifts.

We do not share unless we do all we can as long as we can.

Giving is an outward expression of an inward grace.

Giving is a grace, never a grind.

Sheep give their wool willingly, but did you ever try taking bristles from a hog?

When shearing the sheep, never shear from the rear forwards. They do not want the wool pulled over their eyes.

Our offerings should come from our deposits of faith.

If you would raise money, raise your people first.

True love always prompts a worthy gift.

When we give to the Lord, we are financing a conquest.

Giving is the outpouring of oneself in substance.

Planned giving is happy living.

Our obligations to God are preferred obligations.

We are never to give our bit but our best.

An apple tree doesn't give apples because someone likes to eat them, but simply because it is an apple tree.

Giving the average is what keeps the average down.

What American churches need is "go-givers" as well as "go-getters."

Your heart will not be on the altar unless your money is there also.

The colder a church gets, the more ice cream it takes to keep it going.

You can't feed stewardship with church suppers.

Loving never empties the heart nor giving the purse.

Good stewardship budges and bulges a budget.

Many who go out for the wool come back shorn.

Stewardship is chiefly a way to deepen living, not heighten giving.

A man's reward does not so much consist in what he gets but what he becomes.

III. MONEY

No dust affects the eyes as much as gold dust.

Money often causes hardening of the attitudes.

We used to say that money talks. Now it goes without saying.

Tainted money: 'tain't mine, 'tain't yours.

Some people go to hell with a gold chain about their necks.

A fool and his money are soon spotted.

Dimes used to be big money. Now dimes have changed.

The true test of a man is not how much money he makes but what he makes of his money.

It's much easier to raise a row than to raise revenue.

You cannot serve God *and* Mammon. It's either God *or* Mammon.

IV. MISSIONS

No congregation can afford to build its own "kingdom" at the expense of His kingdom (missions).

We must learn to plead causes, not the cost.

All our missionary causes must be launched on Calvary's tide.

A Christian looks at the needs of the world through the eyes of God.

If missions fail, the rest of us might as well close shop.

We only advance on our knees.

A church which does not reach out will soon pass out.

The first mission box was a cradle.

In the business of missions, prayer comes first. In the business of prayer, missions come first.

Either you are a missionary or a mission field.

Missions and stewardship are Siamese twins.

V. WITNESSING

When witnessing for Christ be sure to put a knot at the end of your line. Seek to win.

The Lord needs witnesses, not lawyers.

Talk to God about your neighbors, and talk to your neighbors about God.

Keep your eyes on the horizon, your feet on the ground, your heart on Christ, and your finger on the door-bell.

VI. SERVICE

Christian service is love in work clothes.

If you would lend a helping hand, look to the end of your arm.

Anyone looking for a soft spot will find it under his hat.

The way to bury your pastor is to keep piling things on him.

After all is said and done, more is said than done.

Pray for a good harvest, but continue to hoe.

God hangs the greatest weight on the smallest wires.

Whom God calls he also qualifies.

Often God's best workmen are found backstage.

You can't kick and pull at the same time.

No one ever does his best. We can all do better.

VII. ORGANIZATION

The average stewardship committee is made up of five people. One does the work, three give him oral support, and one reports what was done to the congregation.

Transmission: Something you pass on to others because you are tired of holding the bag.

Learn from the mistakes of others. You won't live long enough to make them all yourself.

The secret of our weakness is that our plans are so small.

The resources of God are promised only to those who undertake the program of God.

Discretion is the comb we receive from experience after we no longer have any hair to comb.

The cause should never serve organization, but organization the cause.

STEWARDSHIP NUGGETS

Lyle L. Baughman

Stewardship belongs to the center of life and not to its circumference.

It is as great a sin to waste time as it is to waste money.

A will may become a man's folly or his monument.

Real Christian giving is the outflowing of Christian character.

God has a perfect property right to his people.

There can be no true partnership with God unless he has first place in your life.

Love of the right use of money is the root of much good.

Some people shift into reverse when you move from faith to finance or from blessing to budget.

No church is a spiritual success that is a financial failure.

It is a marvel that the church has made progress with so large a portion of its life outside the control of Christ.

Remove stewardship teaching from the New Testament and you leave the gospel in rags and tatters.

An essential part of the Christian education of a child is teaching him to share.

The lips and the purse are often closed by the life.

The only service God seeks is the service of love that responds to his love.

The average church has too many bystanders and not enough standbys.

Man's shrewdest and deadliest enemy is selfishness.

When the church enables men to out-think, out-love, and out-live the world, it demonstrates its right to existence.

A nation that wastes its resources comes at last to waste its very soul.

The speediest way to promote evangelism in the church is to set before its people the challenge of Christian stewardship.

Stewardship and evangelism are the spiritual Siamese twins; to separate them results in the death of both.

It is a misnomer to make a man a disciple without making him a steward.

We are stewards by creation; we determine what kind by our practices.

A Christian steward does not dedicate his time, his talent, his treasure that they may become God's, but because they *are* God's.

Through Christian stewardship we become world citizens in a world brotherhood, with a world responsibility.

Why should anyone hear the gospel twice before everyone has heard it once?

You may excuse yourself from supporting missions if you are willing to relinquish the benefits missionaries brought to your ancestors.

The attempted separation of the gospel of grace from the gospel of giving is the tragedy of modern church life.

The basis of Christian tithing is love for and faith in the Lord Jesus Christ.

The tithe is your pledge that all you have and all you are will be used to the glory of God and the building of the kingdom.

The deeper meaning of the tithe is an honest acknowledgment that all of life belongs to the Lord we serve.

We return a tenth to God in recognition of his divine ownership, but to him belongs the nine tenths also; this he entrusts to us to administer.

When God puts all his resources and power into the Christian partnership, he expects us to acknowledge that all we are and all we have are his.

The money you give is all the money you ever truly save.

Wanted: offering plates for radio and television.

STEWARDSHIP THEMES

Roy L. Smith

At no point is the average individual under a more strict necessity than in the management of money. In these days of easy credit, and installment buying, literally thousands of young people are wrecking their lives as a result of undisciplined financial operations.

To take a Christian attitude toward one's possessions means, first of all, that we possess them instead of being possessed by them.

No man has earned a greater dividend for himself than when he has enslaved himself to a great discipline, for it is the disciplines of our lives that make our livings.

To keep one's soul free from the tyranny of things is one of the greatest achievements to which one can aspire.

Stewardship, in its simplest terms, is a matter of putting God first and forgetting the minors.

Successful living consists of keeping a balance between our wants and our needs, between our pride and our necessity, between our vanity and our deep satisfactions.

God requires differently of every man, but from each man according to his endowment; and from every man something is expected.

Along with the habit of tithing must go the spirit of tithing, to make it all a sacramental thing. If "the gift without the giver is bare," as the poet has said, so it must also be said that the tithe without the spirit of stewardship is bare.

Christian stewardship is not a law, but an attitude; it is not a matter of rule but of reverence.

The decision to invest time, effort, and money in the Church is the most fateful decision any man ever makes. To make that decision in the days of our youth is like putting money into the savings bank and allowing it to produce interest for the rest of our lives.

To decide on a definite, creative, dedicated system of making and spending money is the beginning of wisdom. For as a man manages his possessions, he is very apt to manage his life.

No man is really a success until he has gained the upper hand in the matter of his money, so that he is able to compel it—whether he has little or much—to serve the purposes of his highest possibilities.

It is one of the distinguishing marks of the Christian that he shares with those who have no claim on him.

Financial difficulties, great stress and strain, persecution, dangers, severe opposition, poverty—these have had the effect of bringing out the best and most heroic in religious people. Crises have a way of refining Christians.

The great problem inside the ranks of the Christians is not the matter of giving, but the question of thinking. It is not the lack of funds that hinders the Christian cause, but the lack of convictions concerning possessions.

He who discovers a law of the spirit, such as the principle of stewardship, he discovered something that determines the quality and issues of life. The infinitesimal has as much to teach as the majestic and magnificent.

The greatest impetus some congregations could enjoy would be a crisis that put the people to a test. Complacency is the bitter enemy of achievement.

An aged Negro with a wise heart put the whole matter into a great prayer when he prayed: "O Lord, help me to remember that nothing's going to happen to me today that You and I together can't handle."

Successful living consists of keeping a balance between our wants and our needs, between our pride and our necessity, between our vanity and our deep satisfactions.

Circumstances are the materials out of which we make our lives. Our own spirit is the cement with which we lay up the walls. With the right spirit, we can make out of the circumstances almost anything we desire.

Tithing as a method of giving is not argued as a means of raising money, although it will accomplish that result. Rather, it is offered as a practice which is guaranteed to enhance the spiritual quality of any man's life.

STEWARDSHIP NOTES

Stanley I. Stuber

What would happen if the majority of church members at least tried to follow Christ on a 100% basis day by day? It would certainly be hard on both the individual and the church. But it would also do something radical to both of them. It would create a Christian concern in every community. It would in turn force the community to take the church seriously.

The trouble with most nominal members of the Church is not their doubt of heresy, but their unwillingness to use the gifts of God in the service of others. They do not seem to be willing to put their beliefs to a real test out in the world.

It is now the practice of a President or a cabinet member, when elected, to divest himself of all stocks or financial connections which might tend to influence his judgment. How much more important that the Christian, in his stewardship, get rid of all habits, evil thoughts, associations which might keep him from following Christ all the way!

The strange paradox is that as we accept the heavy yoke of Christ, all our burdens become lighter. As we accept a complete stewardship and give ourselves and all that we have to the Kingdom cause, we become rich. At the very heart of Christian stewardship is the act of service, even at great cost. But the wonderful thing is that Christian service does something to us as well as to the people whom we serve. Stewardship is an act of Christian love.

Christian stewardship helps us to be planters of the good seed. It helps us to know what is good seed; to plant wisely; to cultivate faithfully.

In our Christian stewardship we must be very careful lest we let our tithe of little things be a substitute for giving ourselves fully for great Christian causes.

Stewardship is a matter of keeping "all" of God's commandments. We do not have the right to pick and choose. The good steward is one who is faithful in "all" matters—including the little things and those things he does not like.

Stewardship, if it is to be real and spiritually enriching, must take into consideration vast storehouses of God's riches.

Science has opened up wonderful avenues of discovery, partly in outer space, partly in the physical world in which we live, and partly in our own being. The person who does not accept these new discoveries, who is not willing to adventure, who is not ready to push on from one truth to another, will fail to grasp the glory of God who is still at work in the universe.

If we would only take our stewardship seriously, Christians could once again, as in the first century, turn the world upside down. Yet if they are to do this in the 20th Century they will have to dedicate themselves 100% to the cause of Christ. The time has come to stop thinking about a mere 10%. This ought to be the absolute minimum. What is really needed is a complete, all-the-way consecration to the living and redeeming Master.

STEWARDSHIP LINES

One must be poor to know the luxury of giving.

George Eliot

The greatest grace is a gift, perhaps, in that it anticipates no return.

Longfellow

The wise man does not lay up treasure. The more he gives to others, the more he has for his own.

Lao Tse

We are Goddes stewardes all. Noughte of our owne we have.

Thomas Chatterton, 1752-1770

In giving, a man receives more than he gives, and the more is in proportion to the worth of the thing given.

George Macdonald, 1824-1905

Behold, I do not give lectures of a little charity. When I give I give myself.

Walt Whitman, in LEAVES OF GRASS

The Master Craftsman is trying to make a beautiful and finished product out of pig iron, but the trouble is that we are more pig than iron.

Author Unknown

"Give, not from the top of your purse, but from the bottom of your heart."

David McConaughy

You can live on less when you have more to live for.

Leslie B. Flynn

What a young man earns in the day goes into his pocket; but what he spends in the evening goes into his character.

Theodore L. Cuyler

INDEX

Listing is keyed to illustration number in left margin. Page references are set in italics.